THE FRANCHISE
LEBRON JAMES
AND THE REMAKING OF THE
CLEVELAND CAVALIERS

TERRY PLUTO AND
BRIAN WINDHORST

GRAY & COMPANY, PUBLISHERS
CLEVELAND

To Faith Hamlin,
the LeBron James of agents
—T.P.

To the women in my life,
Mom, Maureen, Kristin, and Alex
—B.W.

© 2007 by Terry Pluto and Brian Windhorst

Gray & Company, Publishers
www.grayco.com

ISBN 978-1-938441-61-5

Printed in the United States of America
v1

CONTENTS

———

CHAPTER 1

"THE KIND OF GUY OTHER TEAMS WANT"

Getting The Guy

A puff of smoke . . .

That's what you see coming from the hands of LeBron James before every game.

A big, white, fluffy puff of dreamy smoke.

It happens when James walks over to the scorer's table seconds before the opening jump ball. He pours resin in his hands, quickly rubs them together, then sends his hands to the heavens, pulling them apart wide as the resin heads to the ceiling. It's the same pregame ritual Michael Jordan performed for years with the Chicago Bulls. Just as Jordan wore No. 23 and had a shoe contract with Nike, so does James. It's a tribute to the player he most admired while growing up in Akron.

On this night, the puff of smoke went up before Game 6 of the 2007 Eastern Conference Finals. The Cleveland Cavaliers were facing the Detroit Pistons at Quicken Loans Arena in downtown Cleveland. Northeast Ohio was in a frenzy, the Cavs one victory away from their first-ever appearance in the NBA Finals. Their first in 37 years. Their first with LeBron James, who was only 22. Their first of many? Some fans dared to dream just that—that this was just the start of something big. Just like the white puff of smoke as James raised his hands and the white power expanded and floated up, up, up and away. Eyes closed, arms fully extended, sound and light and energy pouring over him.

It was as if he and the thirsty fans from his hometown were locked in an embrace.

On this night, something magic would happen. This was more than a basketball game, it was a sports romance. Try to think of another franchise being led out of the sports wilderness by a homegrown player. It would be as if Jordan had come from suburban Chicago instead of Wilmington, North Carolina. Or Larry Bird coming from Boston instead of French Lick, Indiana. Or Magic Johnson being a Los Angeles native rather than growing up in Michigan. Or Mickey Mantle in the Bronx, or Tom Brady in New England. It just doesn't happen, a superstar shouldering the dreams of his hometown as James did that night.

As the smoke rose from James, the fans at mid-court roared. He took it in, maybe not quite believing it all himself. James was born to a teenage single mother and spent much of his youth in the projects and on the streets. He could tell you of guys from his neighborhood who had been shot, guys in jail, guys just lost. He could look under the basket and see his mother, Gloria, in the prime seats, along with his girlfriend Savannah and their young son, LeBron Jr. They are a part of his dream. They'll never be hungry, never have to worry about a place to live, never wonder if someone will shut off the heat or electricity.

Sitting right behind James at mid-court was Dan Gilbert, the owner of the Cavaliers. He watches the games from directly behind the press table—not close to the benches but near the public address broadcaster and those in charge of game presentation: the pregame fireworks, video screen, the sound effects. James is part of *his* dream. A $375 million dream, because that's what he paid for the franchise in 2005—probably twice what it was worth before James joined the team in 2003.

Gordon Gund was listening to this game, and he's a part of the dream, too. He can only imagine what James looked like, muscles rippling, anxious sweat steaming off his forehead as he threw that white powder to the sky. Gund is blind. His eyes at the game are the words of Cavaliers radio broadcaster Joe Tait. This was 2007, nearly 24 years since Gund bought the team from Ted Stepien and saved it for Cleveland. He made that $375 million deal with Gilbert for the sale of the team, but kept 15 percent. He longed to be a part of this night, when the Cavs finally had right guy at the right time.

Basketball is really about getting the right guy.

As Cavaliers veteran point guard Eric Snow once said, "You either have The Guy, or you are trying to get The Guy. In LeBron, we have the kind of guy that other teams want to get."

Getting The Guy . . .

So often, Cleveland fans have seen their guys leave to free agency or trades. Heck, the entire Cleveland Browns *team* left for three years—when Art Modell moved the franchise to Baltimore. Or their teams tried to get the guy, but he turned out to be the wrong guy as happened with the Cavs and Shawn Kemp and Danny Ferry.

But now, Ferry was a part of the dream, too.

After a sometimes frustrating playing career with the Cavs, Ferry is the guy hired by Gilbert to make it work for LeBron James. When Ferry left the team in the summer of 2000, he was respected for his work ethic and his relentless determination to transform himself into a viable NBA player, but he still is known by many Cavs fans as the guy who came in the Ron Harper trade, perhaps the worst deal in franchise history. Now, Ferry is the guy making the trades, and fans were glad to have him back.

Getting The Guy . . .

This night was not about dreams going up in a puff of smoke. It wasn't about a poll in 2006, when ESPN named Cleveland No. 1 in its fan misery index. The fans didn't lose LeBron, perhaps the greatest athlete ever to be born and raised in the working-class neighborhoods of Northeast Ohio. He had just signed a contract extension in summer of 2006, meaning he is committed to the franchise at least until the summer of 2010. He had defied the odds, by not only staying home to play but by overcoming curses and critics to enliven a dying team and inspire a depressed fan base. Every seat in the arena on the mild June night was filled and he was the reason why. They had been filled all season, the Cavs breaking team records for sellouts and overall attendance. Outside, in a large plaza next to the arena, thousands more squeezed in together to watch the game on giant video screens provided by the team. Just four years earlier, the Cavs had attracted the fewest fans in the NBA. Thousands of them were wearing James' replica jersey in an array of colors and perhaps hundreds of thousands more were in bars, in their homes, or even on their jobs doing the same.

Getting The Guy...

Talk to the people selling hot dogs and T-shirts, those who own the restaurants and nightclubs around the arenas—they all will tell you LeBron has made their life better. Not just because he gives fans reason to cheer, but he makes people happy. The team wins, he scores, fans buy stuff—and the vendors make more money than they did before they had The Guy that forever changed this franchise.

Getting The Guy...

Across the court, Marv Albert welcomed a national television audience to the broadcast as James went through his popular pregame maneuver. Before James came, the Cavs hadn't been on national television in more than three years. In the 2006–07 season, more than 50 games were on national TV. As the fans cheered and the cameras recorded, more than 300 media members settled into position to document the historic night, just four years after two of the three newspapers that followed the Cavs stopped even covering their road games due to lack of interest. The side of a nearby building in downtown was covered in a Nike ad for James, a spectacle that was so well received and photographed that the mayor had declared it public art so it could be protected. Dozens more surrounding buildings were covered with signs and banners cheering on the once forgotten team. In a courtside box, the new billionaire owner who had bought new seats for the fans and a new video board to show James highlights on, took in the scene. All of them and more tied together in a package of success and money by the young man's talent and the smile and the puffs of magic smoke.

Getting The Guy...

This was a great night for Nike, the shoe company that won the biggest corporate battle for any amateur athlete to be its company spokesman. Nike bet more than $100 million that there would be days like this, when an 18-year-old from Akron would become one of the NBA's elite players, an international celebrity, a savvy salesman for shoes and clothes. They never said it, but they want him to be their next Jordan, and James was coming off a Jordanesque performance in Game 5 of these Eastern Conference Finals with Detroit, scoring 29 of his team's last 30 points as the Cavaliers prevailed in double-overtime, 109-107. James put 48 points next to his name in the box score that night, and was utterly unstoppable. Jump shots, driving shots, slashing shots and slam dunks. Left hand, right hand—and sometimes, fans swore he did it with no hands. The ball just went from him into the basket. Cavs fans had never seen a performance like this because they never had a player like this. No matter how hard their franchise tried, it was never able to get The Guy.

Then through a white puff of smoke came LeBron James, on to the court, the hearts of fans beating little faster. To Cavs fans, he's their guy—The Guy. Who'd ever have dared dream it?

CHAPTER 2

"WHY WOULD I WANT THIS TEAM?"

LeBron is born . . . and a franchise nearly dies

On the day LeBron James was born, the Cavaliers played in Atlanta—and lost. The score was 109-98 as their record fell to 9-22. As LeBron James was coming into the world on December 30, 1984, born to a 16-year-old mother in Akron, Cavs coach Tom Nissalke was directing a team with a starting lineup of John Bagley, World B. Free, Cliff Robinson, Phil Hubbard and Lonnie Shelton on their way to a 28-54 season. The Cavaliers were a year removed from the Ted Stepien regime and being the most disgraced franchise in the NBA. They wore awful orange uniforms. Their home games averaged 5,075 fans—and that was the announced total; there were often only about 2,500 in the seats. The only reason the Cavaliers were still in business was because Gordon Gund owned the Richfield Coliseum, where the team played. If they moved to another city, Gund would have an empty building.

"It started in 1976 when my brother George owned the Cleveland Barons [of the National Hockey League] and he asked me to join him," said Gordon Gund. "Nick Mileti owned the Cavs. Both of us played at the Richfield Coliseum. By 1977, Chase Manhattan Bank had foreclosed on the building and taken over the Coliseum. We didn't think hockey could make it in the market and we were ready to move the Barons. The bank said they'd give us a significant ownership in the Coliseum if we'd try to keep the Barons there for one more year [1977–78]. We did, but we couldn't draw enough to make it worth our while. We moved the Barons to Minnesota, where they combined with the North Stars."

That left Gund with the Coliseum and the basketball team as the only tenant. By 1981, the bank made a very attractive offer to Gund to take over the general partnership of the Coliseum. Gund had once worked for Chase Manhattan bank, so he understood their business and he knew pro sports from his ownership of the hockey team. He bought the Coliseum for a mere $300,000.

Ted Stepien had bought the Cavs and the team was in the darkest ages of franchise history, which is saying something given the fact the Cavs began their existence in 1970 by losing 15 games in a row. When Stepien owned the team, he made so many terrible trades the NBA put restrictions on the team—all deals had to be approved by the league. It was the first ruling of that type in NBA history. Stepien and his sometimes coach, sometimes general manager Bill Mussel-man, had traded away every first round draft pick from 1982 to 1986. That's five consecutive No. 1 picks. That led to the NBA passing what became the "Ted Stepien rule," which prohibited any franchise from trading first round picks in consecutive seasons. In the three years of Stepien's ownership, the Cavs averaged 5,475; 5,769; and 3,916 fans. No one believed those totals, because tickets were being given away. Often, there were fewer than 1,000 fans in the stands.

"I'd go to those games and I wouldn't hear much of anything," said Gund, who is blind. His hearing is incredibly acute, almost serving as a way to compensate for his blindness. When Gordon Gund didn't hear much, there wasn't much to hear at those games other than the dribble of the ball and squeaking of the shoes on the court.

NBA Commissioner David Stern had come to Gund several times, offering to broker a deal for him to purchase the franchise from Stepien. Stern desperately wanted Stepien out of the league.

"I can get it for you cheap," Stern told Gund more than once.

"Why would I want it?" replied Gund. "There's no way to turn it around. All the draft picks were gone. The reputation of the team in town was awful. It was a mockery. There were more flies than fans in the stands. I'm serious, fewer than 800 on some nights. I knew how many people were really in the building because we owned the build-ing."

Stern thought Gund would be desperate to keep the Cavs in his building. Stern thought wrong. The building cost Gund only $300,000.

"It would not have cost that much to just wrap up [close down] the building," Gund said. "I'd rather do that than buy something [the Cavs] that would just eat my [financial] lunch for years and years. I told the commissioner that we had to have first round picks, or there was no deal."

Gund understood that he was the only possible owner.

"Who else would want it?" he said. "Stepien was threatening to move to Toronto. As I told David, 'Paying anything for this is too much. It's buying the right to lose money for a long time.' And I meant that."

Stern came up with an idea. What if the NBA would sell four first-round picks to the Cavs, replacing four traded away by Stepien? That intrigued Gund because it gave him a way to at least dream the franchise could become competitive. General Manager Harry Weltman also dealt with the league on this issue, and he helped Gund drive a hard bargain to get the picks.

"The owners were reluctant to sell the extra picks, but David convinced them," said Gund. "In the end, it came together."

The league agreed to sell Gund the four picks for about $1 million—about $250,000 each. The deal with Stepien was worth $20 million, but Gund put up only $2.5 million in cash. The $17.5 million was paid out over the next 10 years. He also bought Stepien's lucrative Nationwide Advertising as part of the deal.

If you put the numbers together, by the summer of 1983—only six month before the birth of LeBron James—Gund owned the Cavaliers, the Coliseum and a first round draft pick for 1984, and had spent less than $3 million in upfront money to pull off this deal. Remember, most of the money was paid to Stepien over the next 10 years, and some of that cash came from the profits of Stepien's advertising agency that he had sold to Gund as part of the Cavaliers transaction.

"It turned out great for us," said Gund. "But it was risky, no one knew what would happen back then."

Gund certainly didn't know that the same David Stern who brokered this deal would be announcing about 19 years later that the Cavs had just drafted LeBron James. Or that the man sitting in that TV studio representing the Cavs at the 2003 lottery would be Gordon Gund. Or that the ping-pong ball that bounced just right for the Cavaliers would end up raising value of the Cavs franchise to $375 million. Nor could Gund ever have dreamed anything remotely approaching this financial fairy tale back on December 30, 1984, when he was listening to Cavaliers radio voice Joe Tait describe how his Cavaliers were losing, night-after-night. But hey, at least Ted Stepien was gone.

Gund also didn't know what life would be like for a young LeBron James, because Gund's youth was that of wealth. George Gund, his grandfather, was a beer-maker, and he had the idea of putting bottles in cardboard cases rather than wooden crates, which were more expensive. According to an article in *Smart Business* magazine, George Gund took $130,000 out of his brewery's budget and invested it into something that we know today as decaffeinated coffee. When the Kellogg Company bought it, George Gund pocketed $10 million and the product became known as Sanka. He then moved into the banking business with a company called Cleveland Trust. When his grandfather died, the estate was estimated at more than $600 million. A lot of it was designated to the Gund Foundation, which donates to charities. So making good deals was in the blood of Gordon Gund, just like finding the open man with a pass seems to come as natural to James as breathing or sleeping. But both had to deal with adversity and breaks from life that just aren't fair. When Gund was 30, he went blind from a disease called retinitis pigmentosa. To this day, he's never seen the best player in the history of his franchise.

"But I do have a picture of him in my mind," said Gund. "I have felt his arms and shoulders, and I have a good idea how tall he is in comparison to me. I see strength not just in his body, but his face. I sense he's a very smart, very determined man who just flows up and down the court."

That's a pretty good description of LeBron James, the basketball player. But Gloria James didn't know that when she gave birth at the age of 16. She was young and scared. She has never even officially identified the biological father. Nor has LeBron. A man named Anthony McClelland has called area newspapers and television stations claiming to be James' dad. McClelland was not around much when James was growing up because he spent many years in prison for a variety of charges, including arson. Speculation in Akron is that James' father was a former local basketball star who died not long after leaving high school. Gloria James lived with her mother Freda James during the first few years of LeBron's life in a house on Hickory Street, one of

Akron's bleaker areas. When Freda James died of a heart attack on Christmas Day, 1987, LeBron James was nearly three years old, Gloria James was 19. They began to move from place to place. They lived with friends and relatives, never anywhere for long. LeBron missed a lot of school until he moved in with the family of Frank Walker. That was in the fourth grade. Frank Walker helped coach youth football and basketball teams. In one season of Pee Wee football, James scored 19 touchdowns in six games playing for Walker.

Walker saw Gloria James was struggling with her own personal problems. When it was clear LeBron needed a place to live and a chance to get going in school, he offered to let the 10-year-old James move into his middle class home with his wife and three children. James said he missed 87 days of school in the fourth grade, but none the next year when with the Walkers. Gloria visited often as she worked to pull her life together. With the Walkers, the children were up by 6 a.m. on school days, they had chores, homework had to be done. Rather than rebel, James embraced structure. It was the first sign of what would make him a good teammate and a very coachable star later in life. When James was 12, he moved out of the Walker's home and back with his mother.

There are times when James was asked, "Whose pictures did you have up in your room as a kid?"

He'd always answer, "Michael Jordan."

But it took a long time for him to have a room of his own, because of all the moves. He was Gloria's only child. But there were men to help her, starting with Frank Walker. Then came Dru Joyce II and Lee Cotton, who coached James in various summer league teams and later at St. Vincent-St. Mary.

"As a kid, LeBron liked to shoot the ball—a lot," said Joyce. He said it was common for the other kids to steal the ball from James, whose dribbling skills were raw.

"One day, we were driving down East Avenue [in Akron] and I was telling LeBron about passing the ball, how great players made their teammates better," said Joyce. "I talked to him about getting shots in the flow of the game."

Joyce had no idea how much would stick. James was 11 and not the son of a coach, not a kid who spent his early life hanging around practices with his big brother. "But that was the last time that I ever had to talk to LeBron about shooting the ball too much," said Joyce. "He just got it. He started passing the ball."

It's also when he connected with Dru Joyce III, the son of Dru Joyce II. He was the point guard on a team with Sian Cotton and Willie McGee that became a national AAU power when they were 12-year-olds, winning a national tournament in Orlando. The group would become the core of perhaps the greatest high school basketball team in the history of Ohio. It also would do much to prepare James for the NBA, although no one realized it at the time.

CHAPTER 3

"WHEN YOU TRADE FOR A STAR, THERE'S A RISK . . ."

Shawn Kemp arrives

The Cavaliers really wanted a star. They ended up with Shawn Kemp.

The year was 1997. LeBron James was 12 years old and in the sixth grade, with a Michael Jordan poster on the wall of his Akron bedroom. He was more of a Chicago Bulls fan than a Cavaliers fan because the Bulls had Michael and they won.

The Cavaliers were a frustrating team. They had made the playoffs three times in the previous four years under Mike Fratello—and won a grand total of one postseason game. Barely good enough to get there, not even close enough to stick around in the spring—a 1-9 record in the games that really count, the playoffs.

It had been that way since Lenny Wilkens left in the summer of 1993, back when losing in the second round after a 54-28 record in the regular season was considered a disappointment. That was when Brad Daugherty was healthy, when Larry Nance still had leap in his legs and when Mark Price was the best point guard this franchise had ever seen. It was back when the Cavs were good enough to dream, even if those visions usually ended with a nightmarish Michael Jordan jumper at the buzzer. It was the best of the Richfield Coliseum Era.

But when the Cavaliers gathered in a conference room at Gund Arena in the summer of 1997, the team had just finished their third year in downtown Cleveland. It was the fourth year for Fratello as coach, and his worst with the Cavs: 42-40 record, missing the playoffs. Wayne Embry was the general manager, but that was merely a title, he believed. He said he had lost a power struggle to Fratello, who had gained influence with ownership.

"They were convinced we needed a star," said Embry. "I thought we were on the verge of putting together a pretty good team. We had Terrell Brandon, Chris Mills, Tyrone Hill . . . Bobby Phills was emerging. We had just drafted Vitaly [Potapenko] and Z [Zydrunas Ilgauskas] to give us some size."

This was the Cavaliers first attempt to Get The Guy, the one player who can change an entire franchise.

In Embry's mind, the Cavs didn't have to go star gazing. They just needed more time to develop, more time to draft well, more time to keep adding pieces. He also was convinced they needed another coach, because Fratello's grinding, defensive style never appealed to Embry—even though Embry agreed to hire Fratello after Wilkens departed. The big picture made it appear the Cavs were stuck where no NBA team wants to remain for long—in the middle. Win 40-some games, make the playoffs, lose quick, go home and draft in the middle of the first round. Then do it all over again next year. And next year. And next year. In Fratello's four years, the Cavs had won 47-43-47-42 games. They had watched five-time All-Star center Brad Daugherty retire at the age of 28 with massive back problems. They saw age catch up with Nance, injuries slow Price. They saw an aging Hot Rod Williams traded for a future draft pick, Craig Ehlo leave via free agency and join Lenny Wilkens with the Atlanta Hawks.

These were not even your big brother's Cavaliers.

The excitement sank as the ticket prices rose with the move from Richfield to the new Gund Arena in downtown Cleveland. Embry said when the team left Richfield, ownership did not want to tear down the roster, start over and hope to get lucky in the draft lottery. They wanted to win as many games as possible because they had sold so many luxury suites, and the team was coming off of considerable success at the old Coliseum.

"To be fair to Fratello, we brought him in knowing he was the kind of coach who could perhaps compete for a title," said Embry. "He was not hired to rebuild."

The Cavs tried to do both, which is usually a fatal flaw for any franchise. Either you rebuild, or you play to win. If you try both, you won't do either very well. Attendance peaked in 1994–95, the first year at Gund Arena when the team averaged 20,238. The next season, it was 17,807, then 16,895. The trend was obvious, the luster of the new facility was wearing off as they had only three sellouts. Season tickets were declining, so were sales of luxury suites.

"Trading for Shawn Kemp was purely a business decision," said Embry. "It was about selling tickets, selling suites. We didn't set out to deal for Kemp, I was first told just to find a star who was available and could create some fan interest."

In Embry's mind, this was the worst approach. But he believed he had lost influence with ownership. He also could see the point that the team needed to change something, that another season of 40-some wins and an early playoff exit was looming. While he didn't like the idea of a "star search," he also didn't have a strong counter vision to offer.

"The truth is when you look at almost any championship caliber team, you find a star or two on the roster," said Gordon Gund. "It was more than a business move, it was a practical one. It's hard to get a star, but you have to try. They usually do make your team better."

Gund is correct. The NBA is a star-driven league, more than even baseball or football. One reason is that five play at the same time in basketball, compared to nine in baseball, 11 in football. Actually, it's 22 in football. The point is the fewer athletes who play at one time, the more impact one athlete can have upon the game. That's especially true in a free-flowing sport such as basketball. When Michael Jordan spent a summer as an outfielder in the Class AA Southern League, he discovered that baseball was far more difficult for him than basketball—and not just because fastballs were a 90-mph blur while other pitches curved, sunk and sailed.

"I couldn't tilt the game in my direction," he once said.

In baseball, you have to wait your turn to bat. You have to wait for the ball to be hit to you. You have to wait for the ball to come to you. In basketball, a star can miss a shot, get his own rebound and score. He can have a coach set up plays for him to shoot more than anyone else. Imagine a baseball manager having his best slugger bat 20 times a game, and his light-hitting shortstop never come to the plate. That's basketball. You can highlight your star by giving him many opportunities to glitter and have another player who is never supposed to shoot unless no one else is available because they are covered.

"A star is important, but it has to be the right star," said Jim Paxson, who would take over for Embry as general manager.

But as Gund also asked, "Has a team ever won a championship without a star?"

It's a reasonable question, and the answer is obvious—absolutely not!

You can name a seemingly faceless team such as the 1979 championship Seattle Supersonics coached by one Lenny Wilkens, but they had two young guys named Jack Sikma and Dennis Johnson who'd play in more than a few All-Star games. The recent version of the Detroit Pistons have two star guards in Chauncey Billups and Rip Hamilton, even if they aren't the type of personalities that shoe companies love to feature in commercials. Most championship teams have had guys named Larry Bird, Magic Johnson, Bill Russell and Michael Jordan in the center of their basketball dynasties. Is it possible to find a championship team without a Hall of Famer? Of course. But without any star? No way.

That's why the Cavs went on a star quest, all the while realizing a star doesn't come close to insuring a title—or even a deep drive into the playoffs. But without a star, a team has no chance.

According to Embry, Fratello and his staff rated the top players at each position. Embry said they had Jordan rated first, Shawn Kemp second in the entire league. Kemp was only 27, but had already been in the NBA for eight years as he turned pro out of high school. He was coming off a productive but stormy season in Seattle, averaging 18.7 points, 10.0 rebounds and making his fifth All-Star team. On the surface, he seemed to be in his prime. But he also was available. That's because he feuded with Coach George Karl. He was unhappy with his contract. He had been fined several times. He wanted more money. Karl wanted him out. General Manager Wally Walker wanted to add a less-troublesome player. There were a lot of miles on Kemp's 6-foot-10, 270-pound frame. He came into the league at the age of 18. He was the "Reign Man," because he seemed to reside above the rim. He could run, jump, dunk and seemed to rival Jordan and any other player in terms of sheer God-given athleticism. His shooting and ball handling skills were not star caliber, but he was terrific anyway because of his size, speed and ability to sky. He also had a sensational point guard in Gary Payton setting him up.

After Payton and Kemp led the Sonics to the 1996 Finals where they lost to Chicago, things began to fall apart. That can happen, as players start to worry more about their own agendas and contracts. They believe they were the reason the team had success, and they want to be paid. In the case of Kemp, he already had a contract that had been renegotiated, and he wanted it done again. He was especially upset when the Sonics signed free agent center Jim McIlvaine to a seven-year, $33 million deal—and he averaged a whopping 2.3 points and 2.9 rebounds. The Sonics were desperate for more size, and they overpaid for McIlvaine. The Sonics rejected his request before the 1996–97 season, and he sometimes pouted. He gained weight. He battled with Karl. He seemed distracted and unhappy. He chewed and chewed on the fact that the Sonics had raised Gary Payton's salary to $12 million, and McIlvaine was being paid $3 million. He was only at $3.3 million. But the Sonics had already reworked his contract twice, and he had two years left. They told him to wait a year. He told them to shove it, he didn't want to play in Seattle any more. He was late for practices and flights, had occasions where he seemed disinterested. But he was so gifted, he still was an All-Star.

He also was available.

Embry knew Kemp had problems, lots of problems. Many had been in the newspapers already, such as his struggles with coaches and sulking over his contract. His weight was going up. There was a report of an incident in a bar, and rumors of drinking problems and possibly drug problems. His attitude with Seattle seemed to be that he didn't care where he was traded, it could be Siberia. Just give me a fat, new contract. Embry worked the phones, and helped put together a three-way deal. Milwaukee had an almost-star in Vin Baker, who also was prone to some attitude problems. Seattle had Kemp and his endless list of gripes and issues. Seattle decided that Baker's troubles couldn't be any worse than Kemp's. Turned out, they were close, as Baker also had weight problems and later, drinking problems. The Bucks were glad to dump Baker, but didn't want Kemp.

A former Milwaukee general manager, it was easy for Embry to get in on these discussions. Milwaukee had an interest in several Cavs players, especially Tyrone Hill and Terrell Brandon. These were the kind of players whom Embry loved. He drafted Brandon, traded for Hill. Brandon became an All-Star point guard, replacing Price. But Fratello didn't see the 5-foot-11 Brandon as being talented enough to lift his team to the level of contention. He did average 19 points in his previous two seasons. Hill was a determined power forward, a mechanical player with an inconsistent outside shot. But he loved to rebound. No, he lived to rebound. He rarely worried about his scoring, but averaged 13 points. More important to Embry and the team, Hill delivered 10 rebounds a night despite having limited jumping ability. He did it with his feet on the floor, his elbows out, his butt and back holding off an opponent as he had a knack of establishing excellent rebounding position near the basket. Like most of that Cavs team, Hill squeezed out every drop of talent, but there wasn't much to squeeze.

The deal was in place: Milwaukee would send Baker to Seattle. The Sonics would ship Kemp to the Cavs. The Cavs would trade Hill and Brandon to Milwaukee. Backup point guard Sherman Douglas also would move from Milwaukee to the Cavs. Embry had three pages of information on Kemp. They knew drinking and weight were concerns. They also knew he had some children with different women. There were questions about his motivation. But even 80 percent of Kemp in his prime was still better than any player the Cavs had. At least, that was the theory of most Cavs management.

"In the meetings, they kept saying that when you trade for a star, there's risk," said Embry.

"We knew if Kemp could keep focused, he would be very good," said Gund. "Of course, that ended up being harder than any of us imagined."

Over the years, Gund has gained the impression that Embry has tried to back away from this trade. The owner went around the room and asked everyone if they were for or against the deal. Embry said he saw that everyone but him was in favor, and in the end, he did agree to go along with the trade—albeit reluctantly.

"When I heard it, I knew the trade was a mistake and I doubted it was a deal that Wayne Embry wanted to make," said Cavs broadcaster Joe Tait. "I knew they wanted a marquee player, but you don't want your marquee guy at the city jail. Shawn was great to me, very polite and friendly. But it was no secret that he had problems."

As far as Gund was concerned, when asked, Embry agreed to the deal—and he helped put it together, period. That meant he approved.

"It's interesting how things change over time," said Gund. "Sometimes, people are trying to protect their reputations."

The trade was a blunder on a talent level—they gave up too much in Hill and Brandon—but then the Cavs compounded the felony by immediately presenting Kemp a new contract. They tore up his old Seattle deal, and gave him $100 million over seven years—making him one of the highest paid players in the game. In a sense, they rewarded bad behavior as he forced Seattle to trade him with some stunts very disruptive to the team.

The contract was this:

$8.6 million in 1997–98.

$9.8 million in 1998–99.

$10.8 million in 1999–2000.

$11.7 million in 2000–01.

$12.6 million in 2001–02.

$21.5 million in 2002–03.

$25 million in 2003–04.

When you look at how the contract was backloaded, with the big money in the later years, there's a sense that ownership may have been thinking, *Who knows if we'll own the team four or five years from now. Let someone else pay the guy.*

Embry suggested that ownership put in a weight clause at 265 in the new contract, but they decided to leave it at 275. Kemp showed up at 290 pounds, about 30 over his ideal weight. But the Cavs wanted to keep Kemp happy and decided not to fine him. Here's the irony: the season after the Kemp trade, Embry was voted Executive of the Year, partly because of the trade. He also retooled the team through the draft. He picked Derek Anderson and Brevin Knight in the first round, adding Cedric Henderson in the second round. Embry also acquired veteran Wesley Person in a trade, and 1996 first-round pick Zydrunas Ilgauskas suddenly was healthy, averaging 14 points and 8.8 rebounds in his first pro season on the court. Kemp was dragging around those 25 extra pounds, but still bulled his way to 18 points and 9.3 rebounds, becoming the first Cavalier voted to start in the All-Star game by the fans. The Cavs finished 47-35 with one of the youngest group of players in the league. Despite losing in four games to Indiana in the first round of the playoffs, there seemed to be hope.

In terms of attendance, Kemp did help. The average rose very slightly—only 47 more per game. But the trade stopped most season ticket holders and hardcore fans from drifting away—as seemed to be the case before the trade, according to the Cavs' marketing research.

But the Cavs couldn't maintain it.

Kemp was like too many great athletes. They don't believe they'll ever age. They don't believe they'll ever be injured. They don't understand why everyone is unable to play the game as they do, or why anything about their talent will ever change. Kemp never thought he'd get fat. Even when his waistline kept expanding as his vertical leap was shrinking, he didn't believe it. He acted like his bathroom mirror was one of those distorted ones in a funhouse—*That can't really be me.*

He never thought it would be so hard just to run down the court—or to leap above the rim. He never thought he'd tire so fast, or have to work so hard just to lose any weight. He never thought he'd commit so many fouls, have so many shots blocked or have so many balls just bounce off his fingers. He never thought he'd be anything but an athlete in his middle 20s who was one of the purest athletes the NBA has ever seen. He certainly never understood what it meant to be a truly great player for a long time.

For too many athletes, the off-season is just that—time off.

They may play pickup basketball, lift a few weights and perhaps run some laps—but they don't take it very seriously. They believe they deserve a break from the physical demands of the season. After six months of 82 games, plus training camp, plus the playoffs, they figure they deserve a break. Besides, they made millions of dollars. Time to head to Las Vegas or Atlantic City, hit the casinos and the restaurants.

But the stars who have long careers seldom spend much of their summers in lengthy pickup games. They hire personal trainers. They watch their diets. They lift the right weights to stay strong, but lean. They work on individual parts of their games. Michael Jordan once spent most of his summer workouts in the gym, alone, dribbling around chairs with his left hand—because he discovered that he was driving too often to his right. Another summer, he worked on a 3-point shot from the top of the key. Yet another summer, it was low post moves—a little fall-away jumper—near the basket. His goal was to come back with something new every year to attack the defenses that continually were evolving to try and stop him.

Magic Johnson spent a summer practicing a strange one-handed set-shot from 3-point range. He discovered that defenses believed he could not make a shot from beyond 15 feet. He never had a reliable jumper, so he went back to the basics—a one-handed set shot: the ball on his finger tips, wrist cocked at a 90-degree angle, then a straight, quick follow-through as he released the ball. Johnson never became a great 3-point shooter, but it was another weapon available. But that wasn't enough for the Lakers star. He was intrigued by Kareem Abdul-Jabbar's hook shot. It was unstoppable, and Magic begged his superstar teammate to teach him the sky hook. While Johnson's hook was never as pretty or shot from as high above his head as Jabbar's, it was a shot he could use inside. By the end of his career, the hook—like Jordan's little fadeaway jumper—became his most feared shot. And neither player had those shots when they began their pro careers.

Kemp didn't follow any of these examples, despite being told by coaches. When questions about his weight were raised, he simply pointed to his stats—he still averaged close to 20 points and 10 rebounds per game. He still was an All-Star, still a productive player. What's the problem, those extra pounds really didn't seem to hurt, right? In the playoffs, he averaged 26 points and 10 rebounds as the Cavs lost to Indiana in four games. So what if he fouled out of 15 games, most in the NBA. He was a physical presence inside. He may have been bigger, but he was still better than anyone in a Cavs uniform.

But the front office feared Kemp would continue to pack on the pounds, that it would eventually weigh down his game. They had six years and nearly $92 million left on his original $100 million contract—they wanted him ready to play well for a long time. They asked him to stay close to the team after that first 1997–98 season in Cleveland so they could help him get in shape and monitor his weight. Kemp had little interest in that. The summer was his time, and he'd earned the rest. Privately, the Cavs feared what that would mean to his already growing girth and could lead to injuries, but publicly they said Kemp was a veteran, and he knew what was best for him.

Then came the lockout at the start of the 1998–99 season as the players and owners battled over a new labor contract. There would be no training camp. Players were not allowed to work out with coaches or members of the franchise. There were rumors the season might ever start as the labor battle dragged on, seemingly with no end in sight. Kemp wasn't the only player who developed a disdain for conditioning during the lockout, but he became the worst offender. When play did resume on February 5, 1999, Kemp was *huge.* The Cavs tried to hide it, but he weighed in at 318. That was 28 more pounds than the previous season—and they considered him at least 20 pounds overweight at the time of the trade.

After the promising 1997–98 season with the 47-35 record, the Cavs sank to 22-28. Kemp somehow averaged 20 points, but he was slow, foul-prone and too often late for team flights and practices. He was 28, but looked closer to 38.

In the summer of 1999, two years after the Kemp deal was supposed to revive the franchise, owner Gordon Gund fired both Wayne Embry and Mike Fratello. Embry was to remain as an "advisor" to new general manager Jim Paxson. Embry had a year left on his contract, but Gund said when he decided to fire Fratello, it also made sense to move up the switch from Embry to Paxson. Gund hired Paxson in 1998 with the idea that he'd learn from Embry for two years, then take over the team.

The new NBA labor agreement brought in the luxury tax, a penalty if a team exceeded the salary cap. It's a bit more complicated than this, but the basic concept is if the salary cap was set at $50 million—and your payroll is $60 million—you must pay $10 million to the league in a luxury tax. It's the luxury of going over the salary cap. There are exceptions that allow teams to go through the cap without penalties, but the Cavs were looking at being a team over the cap as Kemp's salary continued to rise each year.

"We did not want to be capped out [and pay a luxury tax]," said Gund. "He also had to find a way to get better, and we had to get rid of some of our longer contracts of players we knew would not be with us when we were making a run at a championship."

Gund remains sensitive about the Kemp deal, and he still wants fans to know it wasn't only his idea: "When things go well, a lot of people take credit. When they don't, it's ownership's fault."

The one guy in the front office who was blameless for this was Paxson, who inherited Kemp along with the stricter salary cap rules. As the Cavs were heading into the year 2000, the franchise was sinking under the weight of Kemp and other decisions made by ownership and the front office.

"After the collective bargaining agreement was signed, there were three years before the luxury tax went into effect," said Paxson, meaning the Cavs had to get rid of Kemp's contract by 2002 or face major financial consequences.

The 1997–98 team that won 47 games had fallen apart by 2000. Kemp was getting fatter. Ilgauskas suffered a major foot injury and no one knew if he'd ever play again. Brevin Knight was developing knee troubles. Cedric Henderson went from a promising 10-point scorer as a rookie to an invisible man. He could play stretches of 15-to-20 minutes and not even take a shot or grab a rebound.

"We had to start chopping contracts, not just Kemp's," said Paxson. "We feared we'd be a mediocre team and a tax-paying team."

That was the worst of both basketball worlds. Paxson started dealing with players such as Bob Sura and Wes Person, who had long-term deals. He also had to somehow get Kemp to play at a reasonable level.

"After the lockout, he may have been up to 330 pounds," said Paxson. "One year, he came in at 315 or 320. He'd get his weight down to 290, and the media would say he was getting in shape, but he was still too heavy. To me, it was amazing he could play at all."

Like Wayne Embry before him, Paxson talked to Kemp. Like Embry, he found Kemp to be very engaging and polite. He'd promise to change, "saying all the right things," explained Paxson. "I think in his heart, he meant it. But he didn't have the character and background to [change]."

In one meeting with Kemp, Paxson said Gund had two 25-pound weights waiting for the team's highest paid player. He told Kemp to pick up the weights, and said, "Shawn, this is what you're carrying around on your body right now."

It was a very vivid show-and-tell lesson, and Kemp promised to take it to heart and take in less when he sat down for dinner. But it was like so many of his other promises. He meant it when he said it, but forgot it later. The Cavs also were certain Kemp had a drinking problem. They suspected some drug use because he was chronically late. The team was losing. In Paxson's words, "After the lockout, fan interest was almost non-existent. You couldn't sell tickets, you couldn't give them away. No one was coming to the games."

CHAPTER 4

"HE WAS THAT GOOD"

LeBron James on the rise

When LeBron James played his first high school basketball game on December 3, 1999, it was in a half empty gym in Cuyahoga Falls, a suburb of Akron. James was starting as a freshman for St. Vincent-St. Mary High School. Most high school fans were paying far more attention to the state football finals that evening, which included Walsh High, a local Catholic school. But there was one college coach in the stands. Bob Huggins had been the head coach at University of Akron. In 1999, he was at the University of Cincinnati, and he'd heard about a ninth grader named LeBron James. Of course, Huggins had heard of so many high school freshmen who were supposed to be the next Michael Jordan, the next Julius Erving. Most were lucky to even start for Division I college teams.

But once in a while, someone comes along . . .

And just in case, Huggins wanted to be there, right from the start.

Before the game, St. Vincent-St. Mary coach Keith Dambrot was nervous because he was starting three freshmen, including James. Dambrot had been a college coach at Tiffin, Ashland University and Central Michigan. He was not a naïve young man in his first coaching position. Nor was he prone to praising players, especially freshmen. But he raved about James to California coach Ben Braun, a close friend from when Braun was the head coach at Eastern Michigan and Dambrot was an assistant.

"He'll certainly play Division I, and he may even be good enough just to go straight to the pros," Dambrot said before James' first high school game.

That first night, James was a lanky, 6-foot-3 forward who actually looked like a high school kid. He didn't need to shave. He seemed a bit uncomfortable on the court, wanting to fit in with some older teammates. He scored 15 relatively easy points, most of them on fast break situations in the flow of the game. His high school team would finish that season at 27-0. James would average 18 points that season, shooting 51 percent from the field and a stunning 79 percent at the foul line. That was his highest free throw percentage of any year in high school, or the pros. It was in the state tournament where James broke loose. In one game, he scored 15 points to begin the second half. In the two final games at Value City Arena on the Ohio State campus, he scored a total of 44 points while shooting 16-of-22 from field. He also had 20 rebounds in those two games.

During the season, Coach Ben Braun scouted James, and then told Dambrot, "He'll never play in college, he's too good."

The national coming out party was the famed Five-Star basketball camp run by legendary summer league coach Howard Garfinkel for more than 35 summers. Name a great player, and he probably has passed through Garfinkel's camp. ESPN's Dick Vitale rated James among the top five sophomores in the country. In *ESPN The Magazine*, Vitale wrote, "James is a tall, athletic point guard with serious skills and a brilliant first step." *The Sporting News* said James was the second-best sophomore in the nation.

All of this came after James was at the Five-Star camp.

In the summer of 2000, Garfinkel didn't care that James' high school team was 27-0, that it won the Ohio Division III title that spring, or that James had 25 points, nine rebounds and shot 8-for-11 in the championship game. Garfinkel had even higher standards, a historical perspective. In an interview with the *Akron Beacon Journal*, Garfinkel talked about the 100-plus NBA players who have attended his Five-Star camp—names such as Grant Hill, Stephon Marbury, Rasheed Wallace, Christian Laettner, Elton Brand, Dell Curry and Bobby Hurley.

"You heard all those NBA guys I mentioned?" said Garfinkel. "LeBron played as well or better than any one of them when they were sophomores at my camp. It was ridiculous; he totally dominated. I've never seen anything quite like it."

How so?

"In the middle of the week, we had some guys hurt in our NBA [high school junior and senior division], and we moved him up," Garfinkel said. "He was playing four games a day, with both the sophomores and our NBA divisions. He made both all-star teams, both of them, in his own division and the NBA division. In the 35 years that I've had this camp, that's never happened before. He can shoot it. He can pass off the dribble. He knows the game. He seems like a great kid. Like I said, I don't want to say too much, but I like this kid a lot. I don't want something to happen to him."

When Garfinkel said this, James was only 15 years old.

At 15, his friends teased him about his big ears and he talked trash about their teeth or their feet. But at 15, he'd already played summer basketball in Utah, in Memphis, in Las Vegas, in Pittsburgh, and, believe it or not, in Milan, Italy. James talked about a stretch that summer where he had attended camps in Pittsburgh, Orlando and Tennessee. "I was gone almost all July," he said. He sounded like a weary businessman saying next summer he plans to cut down on his travel schedule. That's because all the camps and tournaments wanted a piece of LeBron James. They wanted a seat, even in the caboose, just in case his train carried him all the way to the NBA. At 15, James had people telling him he'd be the next Kobe Bryant or Tracy McGrady—the next kid to go right from high school to the pros. And he had pictures of them in his room. But his favorite player was Michael Jordan. He even told everyone that he was 6-foot-6½, because that is Jordan's exact height. Jordan is the perfect role model for James, and not just because he is arguably the greatest basketball player ever. Those pictures on the wall of James' room demonstrate the war for this young man's soul. Would he be like Jordan, who waited for the game and fame to come to him and became the greatest marketer and most popular player in NBA history? Or like Bryant and McGrady, who went directly from the senior prom to the NBA, and didn't exactly endear themselves to fans and coaches as Jordan did.

"I try not to think about that stuff," James said at 15. "I have Dick Vitale's magazine on the wall of my room. To see my name there, I want to live up to that. It's like Dick Vitale invented college basketball, you know what I mean?"

To a 15-year-old reared on Vitale screaming about "Diaper Dandies" on ESPN, maybe the bald former coach of the University of Detroit did start college basketball. Or at least, Vitale helped make it what it is today: an industry where 15-year-olds like James are rated and then dated by the top colleges and even the pros.

More than 100 colleges had written James. The coaches couldn't talk to him until his junior year, but they all knew his name. Coaches from Michigan State, Duke, North Carolina, California, Ohio State—virtually every major basketball school in the country—were in contact with coach Keith Dambrot, telling him of their interest in James.

At 15, LeBron James sometimes felt 35. He knew big money was not far away, and he knew his family, namely his mother Gloria, needed support.

"LeBron keeps telling me that soon I won't have to worry about a thing," Gloria James said in 2000. "I'll have a house, a car, everything paid for. I tell him to take his time. I tell him that I don't need those things. My dream is to have my own chef, because I love to eat."

"He was like a child prodigy," said Dru Joyce III, who played with James starting in the fifth grade and all through high school. "It's like they talk about Mozart doing all those symphonies when he was young. LeBron was always bigger and better than everyone else. He never went through a stage where he was clumsy. He grew, and he always had those muscles."

In the seventh grade, James was 5-foot-8.

When he enrolled in high school, he was 6-foot-2.

Heading into his sophomore season, he was 6-foot-6, oops, make it the Jordan-like 6-foot-6½. His arms seemed to hang down to his knees. His hands were huge, his fingers long and delicate. His body flowed like a river, and his rangy legs seemed to cover the court in but a few incredible strides. Despite the growth spurts, he's never endured one of those uncoordinated stages where arms and legs refuse to function in harmony. His grade-point average was a 2.8, which is a B-minus. His freshman English teacher, Jake Robinson, said James "has excellent penmanship and wrote some nice essays. He still has to work on his writing, but he cares about it."

"I never had to spank LeBron, not even once," Gloria James said. "When I tell him something, he listens."

That's because James truly loves and appreciates his mother. He talked about the hard times, especially when he was in the fourth grade and they "moved from place to place to place" because of money problems. "My mother is my mother. But she also is my sister, my brother, my best friend, my uncle, my everything," he said, mentioning he has a tattoo on his arm, a woman with the name "Gloria," his way of honoring his mother.

In the fall of 2000, James decided to play football, catching 42 passes, 14 for touchdowns. Former Ohio State assistant football coach Lee Owens scouted James, and confided to friends that James could play receiver in the Big Ten right now—and this was when he was still a 15-year-old high school sophomore,

"I first saw LeBron play in the seventh grade, and I knew he'd play great in high school," said Dambrot. "As a freshman, he averaged 17 points and shot 50 percent for me. He could have averaged 25. But he wanted to fit in. As a freshmen, I knew he'd play Division I college basketball. Early in his sophomore year, I knew that he'd never get to college. He was going to turn pro. He was that good."

CHAPTER 5

"THEY NEVER WOULD HAVE BEEN ABLE TO REBUILD"

Shedding Shawn Kemp

Jim Paxson was frantically trying to trade Shawn Kemp in summer of 2000. But first had to cut a road through a salary cap jungle and a decade of mediocre basketball so that the Cavs would be bad enough to eventually become a good team. That's how it works in the NBA. Before you go up, you usually have to go down.

Way, way, way down.

"In almost every meeting we had that season, it was 'Do you think you can trade Kemp?'" recalled Paxson. This was just three years after every summer meeting with ownership beginning, "How can we get a star?"

Paxson talked to lots of teams, and found no interest. Word of Kemp's personal problems had spread, and rumors of everything from drinking to drug use were common in NBA circles. A *Sports Illustrated* story about athletes having out-of-wedlock children highlighted Kemp, who was said to have seven children with six women. It was just awful publicity for the Cavaliers, and certainly made it even harder for Paxson to find a taker for Kemp. It wasn't so much about morality, but reality. If the guy has so little discipline to have so many children with so many different women, how will he ever get in shape? That's the kind of questions asked behind the closed doors in NBA front offices.

Then Paxson talked to Bob Whitsitt, general manager of the Portland Trail Blazers. He was the general manager of the Seattle Supersonics who gambled by drafting Kemp in the first round—the No. 17 pick—in the 1989 draft. Kemp was already considered a troubled soul. He was supposed to play at Kentucky, and even enrolled at the university. But there were problems, he never suited up for a game—then transferred to Trinity Valley Junior College in Texas. But he never played there, either. So Whitsitt drafted a high school kid who went to two colleges, yet played at none. Took him in the first round. Sonics fans booed. Many experts doubted Kemp would be mature enough to make an impact. But Whitsitt told reporters, "Had Shawn gone to school, he would eventually be the No. 1 pick in the entire draft."

It was dangerous to hype such a young inexperienced player like Kemp, but Whitsitt became a prophet. It took a few years, but Kemp became an All-Star. Seattle went to the 1996 NBA Finals. Whitsitt had left Seattle in 1994 after a battle with ownership, and took over as general manager in Portland. He was Paxson's boss in the late 1990s, and Paxson knew Whitsitt was a Kemp fan. If any general manager would be willing to take a chance on Kemp at this stage of his career, it was Whitsitt, who believed that he knew Kemp well enough to convince him to get in shape.

"The talks started not with Kemp, but with Brian Grant," said Paxson.

Grant was a power forward in Portland, a rugged rebounder and not much of a scorer. He had become a free agent, and Paxson was checking up on Grant by talking to Whitsitt. Portland had some interest in Cavs guard Andre Miller. The Cavs would trade their young, promising point guard for future draft picks and some veterans near the end of their contracts to create salary cap room. Paxson also was interested in a bigger deal, involving Brian Grant.

"Bob kept telling me that he wanted to keep Grant," said Paxson. "He also asked me about Kemp. Portland had just lost in the seventh game of Western Conference Finals. They were up 15 points on the Lakers, but couldn't hang on. The Lakers had Shaq [Shaquille O'Neal] and Portland was thinking they needed a big guy to battle Shaq inside."

Since Paxson and Whitsitt knew each other so well, Paxson was compelled to tell his old boss: "I'm sure you're aware of the problems that Shawn has. I'm not about to tell you that he's changed."

Paxson didn't tell Portland that the Cavs had enforced the 275-pound weight clause in Kemp's contract during the 1999–2000 season.

He paid about $300,000 in fines. It didn't matter. He kept eating, kept being late, kept being Shawn Kemp. That $300,000 seemed like $300 to him, no big deal. The rest of the numbers were open to the public, from the four years and $70 million left on the contract to the league-leading 371 personal fouls to the career-low .417 shooting percentage. To somehow squeeze Kemp's massive contract into the tight belt of the salary cap, the idea was for the Blazers to sign Grant to a big contract—then trade him to the Cavs for Kemp. Since Grant had played at Xavier University in Cincinnati, the hope was he'd be willing to return to Ohio. No way, said Grant's agent. Grant wanted to play for a contender, and the team on the shores of Lake Erie was miles away from even making the playoffs.

"Miami was talking to Mark Bartelstein [Grant's agent] about signing him, and Grant was very interested in playing for the Heat," said Paxson. "Portland still wanted Kemp. I wanted to get Kemp traded, almost at any price for nearly anyone. They were thinking that they had a lot of good players, Kemp would not have to average 20-10 [20 points, 10 rebounds]. They also had an assistant named Tim Grgurich, who had been close to Kemp when he worked in Seattle."

For three weeks, Paxson worked on this trade as the middle man.

Miami wanted Grant.

Grant wanted Miami.

Portland wanted Kemp.

Paxson wanted Kemp out of Cleveland.

Portland and Miami were not a good salary cap match.

"Bob [Whitsitt] was ready to take a big swing [for a title] and trade for Shawn," said Paxson. "He also was preparing to take his family on a vacation to Africa, which they had planned for years. It was early August, and Whitsitt was getting ready to leave on vacation. I knew if we didn't get an agreement in place before he left, we'd probably never get it done."

That's because the longer any general manager thought about trading for Kemp—and the more people he consulted about it—the less sense it made because of the big dollars involved. So Paxson was frantically on the phones, talking to Heat General Manager Randy Pfund, Whitsitt and Bartelstein, who was Grant's agent. In the Cavs offices, team attorney Dick Watson was working on the salary caps of all three teams, creating scenarios for a trade to work. This was Watson's specialty, as he was recognized as one of the NBA's best at manipulating and stretching salary caps. The Cavs were in overdrive, the feeling a desperation knowing that this could be their own shot to get rid of Kemp. No matter what it took, *they had to get it done.* The pressure Paxson felt was enormous. He had to *make it work.* The immediate future was riding on these talks, perhaps even the long term. *Do it now,* thought Paxson. *Don't let Bob take any more time to think about it.*

Those words were *pounding* inside his head.

Paxson also felt a bit helpless. He couldn't *make* Portland take Kemp. He couldn't *make* Miami sign Grant. He couldn't *make* Grant agree to go to the Heat, especially if another team came out of nowhere and tried to sign him. He couldn't do much of anything but keep all the parties talking, keep everyone focused. Buy some time as Watson had his computer, *running . . . roaring . . . spitting out* page after page of salary cap trade possibilities. There was something else Paxson had to do—get some players from Miami in return to make sure the Heat could clear cap room to sign Grant. Three years later—during the LeBron Lottery of 2003—Gund, Paxson and the rest of the Cavs would experience this same type of heart-pounding, mind-numbing pressure. The difference was that was luck, and bouncing ping-pong balls., Nothing they could do about it.

But this, this was scary. *What if it didn't work?*

Every time Paxson thought about that, he shoved it out of his mind. There's a great line in the movie *Apollo 13* where the actor Ed Harris bellows, "Failure is not an option," as the scientists scheme to bring home the astronauts and their failing space ship. While it was not actual life and death taking place in Paxson's office at Gund Arena, it felt like his professional life was at stake. He knew if he could not get rid of Kemp, his dreams and prayers and hopes of putting together a winner was doomed—strangled by an ever-tightening salary cap from Kemp's contract. Watson found two players on short contracts whose contract numbers would help Miami create room to sign Grant—the names were Clarence Weatherspoon and Chris Gatling. Two journeymen who had been forwards for several teams. Weatherspoon was a quiet, hard-working undersized forward at 6-foot-7. Gatling was a shoot first, shoot second and forget defense forward who bounced from team to team to team. Former Cavaliers Player Personnel Director Gary Fitzsimmons used to call him "The Gatling Gun" because he was such a shameless shooter. Gatling could be a bit difficult to coach, but Paxson didn't care. In fact, he was glad to get Weatherspoon, a good guy. At least there was some talent in the deal. More importantly, the numbers worked on the salary cap.

What convinced Portland to take Kemp was a meeting between Whitsitt, Kemp and Kemp's agent, Tony Dutt. As he was when confronted by the Cavs with their concerns, Kemp was friendly, charming, insisting he'd do better. After three depressing years in Cleveland, the idea of returning to the Northwest, to playing in Portland and for Whitsitt—the man who showed the most faith in Kemp by drafting him—had Kemp ready to say and promise almost anything to make it happen. Whitsitt had to know there was a part of Kemp that could not be taken seriously. But Whitsitt was there in the beginning, too. Whitsitt put his reputation on the line by drafting Kemp. Like a guy who didn't know when to walk away from the poker table with his winnings, Whitsitt went back for more—he went all the way—and traded for Kemp, assuming the entire contract.

We're talking four years . . . and seventy million . . . off the books!

Paxson tried not to think about that for long, but he knew he could never find another general manager . . . another team . . . another owner . . . willing to take such a huge gamble on Kemp.

"We'll do it," said Whitsitt

Here's how it finally worked:

The Cavs sent Kemp to Portland.

Portland sent a retiring Gary Grant (no relation to Brian Grant) to the Cavs to ease room on their salary cap. Portland signed Brian Grant to a staggering seven-year, $87 million deal, and then shipped him to Miami.

Miami shipped Gatling, Weatherspoon and a 2001 first-round pick to the Cavs.

"I couldn't believe they found anyone to take Shawn," said former general manager Wayne Embry. "If they don't make the trade—and especially since they didn't have to take big contracts back—they never would have been able to rebuild. But they also may have won just enough games with Kemp to stay out of the upper level of the lottery, and that means no LeBron."

Paxson correctly believes that this deal set the stage for the arrival of James, for him "lighting up Cleveland like Vegas," as he promised he would on lottery night.

"This deal worked out even better than the first one that I had in mind," said Paxson.

That's because Brian Grant's contract could have been as destructive as Kemp's. Not only was it worth $87 million over seven years, he was not even close to a star. Grant was a blue-collar, hit-the-boards rebounder. He didn't shoot well from the outside. He was just a so-so scorer. At the time of this trade, Grant was 28 and had averaged 11 points and 8.5 rebounds for his career. In his last season with Portland, Grant averaged 7.3 points, 5.5 rebounds in 21 minutes a game off the bench. Every summer, some average free agent (usually a big man) inspires a couple of star-starved teams to toss millions in their direction, as if paying them like superstars will make them superstars. Before Grant, players such as Jon Koncak and former Cavalier Hot Rod Williams cashed in, Williams one year earning more than Michael Jordan.

In the summer of 2000, the lucky man was Brian Grant, but even more important, the Cavs were the luckiest team.

Kemp's career would collapse in Portland. He grew fatter. He had drug problems and was twice suspended. He finally walked out on the last two years of his contract because of his personal problems and gave up at least $16 million.

"In the summer [of 2006], I was working with my brother [Bulls GM John Paxson] in Chicago," said Paxson. "Shawn's agent called and said Shawn was in shape and wanted to play again. He was only 35, and we figured why not take a look at him? It wouldn't cost us anything. So we agreed."

Paxson paused as he told this story . . .

"But Shawn never showed up," he said in a soft voice. "It's just sad."

CHAPTER 6

"NONE OF US SHOULD WORRY ABOUT RECRUITING HIM"

LeBron makes a splash

During the same summer of 2001 when Jim Paxson was desperately trying to trade Shawn Kemp, LeBron James was a phenom at age 16. His St. Vincent-St. Mary High School team won its second consecutive state title. James was named the top high school basketball player in Ohio, a remarkable honor for a sophomore. His team was 51-1 in James' first two seasons, the only loss being 79-78 to the nation's top-ranked Oak Hill Academy, a game where James scored 33 and was named the game's MVP. In the final minutes, he missed two free throws, an open jumper near the foul line and a 3-pointer at the final buzzer.

Not that the estimated 20 NBA scouts cared. On the surface, they were at the game in Columbus, Ohio, to see a kid named DeSagana Diop, a 7-foot senior from Oak Hill. Word was the import from Senegal was headed to the 2001 NBA draft. But scouts came away talking about James, marveling at how he was so physically mature, so powerful at 6-foot-6, 220 pounds and only 16 years old. He looked like an NBA player the moment he stepped on the court. His game was surprisingly refined for his age, and it showed against top prep competition. More than a dozen players have passed through Oak Hill en route to the NBA. It's a prep school in Mouth of Wilson, Va., where the average class size is 10. Students come from across the country. About 100 attend the school, nearly all are boarding students. In the case of basketball, it's a finishing school for major college prospects who need to raise their grade point averages or standardized test scores to qualify for a Division I scholarship. Or there were players who had trouble in their hometowns and it was deemed a good idea for them to spend a year in the Blue Ridge Mountains away from the lure of the streets and bad company. Nearly every year since the middle 1980s, Oak Hill has been among the nation's top five high school teams, sending such players as Jerry Stackhouse, Josh Smith, Steve Blake, Jeff McInnis, Stephen Jackson, Ron Mercer, Rajon Rondo and Carmelo Anthony to college and then the pros. Texas star Kevin Durant also played there for a year while in high school.

Despite James' inability to win that Oak Hill game, the fact that he scored 33 points against a team of seniors headed to top colleges was impressive. So was the willingness of James—a sophomore—to take those clutch shots, even if he missed. He played like a senior. After the game, veteran Oak Hill coach Steve Smith said, "He's just about impossible to stop one-on-one. He has some future ahead of him."

In Northeast Ohio, there already was a sense of wonder—what if James could somehow end up with the Cavaliers? At 16, he was being considered a savior to a franchise that just seemed intent on dumping Kemp and other high-salaried players.

As a sophomore, James averaged 25.6 points, 7.5 rebounds, 7.0 assists.

"He doesn't have to score to feel good about himself," St. Vincent-St. Mary coach Keith Dambrot told the Associated Press when James won the 2001 Ohio Player of the Year award. Here are a few other nuggets from that old story. The two runners-up for the award were Mike Gansey and J.J. Sullinger. Gansey went to St. Bonaventure, then transferred to West Virginia. Sullinger attended Ohio State. The Associated Press also said James was considering four colleges: Ohio State, North Carolina, Michigan State and California.

Looking back on that story five years later, Dambrot laughed and said, "Early in his sophomore year, I knew LeBron would never go to college. He had the grades, but he was just too good. The college coaches who were checking him out were telling me the same thing. They loved LeBron and wanted him, but no one thought he'd go to college."

That was especially true when James attended the ABCD summer camp in 2001. Like the Five-Star camp and a few others, it is a summer showcase for the nation's top high school players. College coaches pack the gyms to watch possible recruits strut their stuff and compete against other blue chippers from coast to coast. The ABCD camp was in Hackensack, N. J. This was held right after the 2001 NBA draft, and four of the top eight players selected came straight from high school. The No. 1 pick was Kwame Brown, personally scouted and selected by Michael Jordan, who was president of the Washington Wizards. The Bulls pulled off a trade and ended up with two high school big men— Tyson Chandler and Eddie Curry. Picking eighth, the Cavs grabbed Diop, the kid who played for Oak Hill against James—and had only a dozen points in that game, looking heavy and very raw. He had been in the U.S. for only two years. But he was a hefty 7-foot, breathing, and the Cavs were desperate for size as they were trying to trade Kemp and worried that 7-foot-3 Zydrunas Ilgauskas would never come back from a major foot injury that had required several surgeries.

James believed he was better than any of those top picks. The ABCD Camp was played in the Rothman Center, a cramped gym on the campus of Fairleigh-Dickinson University. There were only two courts that were on actual hardwood, the rest were on a rubberized sport-court. This is where Sonny Vaccaro set up the tournament. Vaccaro has long been a summer league power-broker, a man who has represented shoe companies such as Nike and Adidas. In the summer of 2001, Vaccaro was working for Adidas. He had lots of access to James and other premier players so he could sell them on the benefits of signing a shoe deal with Adidas once they turned pro. Convincing James to come to his camp was a major coup for Vaccaro, because his ABCD camp was taking place roughly at the same time as Nike's camp in Indianapolis for the top high school players. This was just one example of the different battles between shoe companies for the attention of James while he was still in high school. College coaches were flying between Indianapolis and Newark so they could catch the top players at both camps.

Dressed in the same dark blue and gold uniform with the same shoes and socks as 232 other teen-agers, the 16-year-old James seemed to blend into the crowd. In his last high school game, James led his team to a second consecutive Division III state title in front of the first sellout for a high school game in the history of Columbus' Value City Arena with more than 17,000 fans. Since then, he had added an inch of height and about 10 pounds, making him 6-foot-7 and close to 230.

He also was the center of international speculation that he might do what no high schooler has done. Somewhere in between an article in *Slam* magazine and a column in the *New York Times* by Ira Berkow, James sparked a debate when he indicated he had an interest in becoming the first to try to leave high school early and jump to the NBA.

That's right, turn pro after his junior year.

"It's something that I have to consider," James told reporters at the ABCD camp. "I try not to think about it and just concentrate on what I'm here to do."

One theory was James could play his junior year, then drop out of school to play for money in Europe in the winter of 2002–03, waiting to be eligible for the 2003 NBA draft. It was at this 2001 ABCD camp that the speculation of James turning pro so young gained credibility. He shut down the MVP of the 2000 ABCD Camp, Lenny Cooke, holding him to nine points. James scored 24 points of his own including a game-winning 3-pointer at the buzzer. He joined past winners Kobe Bryant and Stephon Marbury as the camp's MVP. Suddenly, the question of who was the best high school player in the nation was answered. The fans were at one side of the gym, the college coaches were on the other side—which was roped off because the coaches were not allowed to talk to the players. According to NCAA rules, this was a "non-contact period." But the coaches wore their school shirts and made sure the players saw them—especially the top stars such as James. But the media, autograph seekers, strange street agent types and others could mingle with the players, and there was little supervision. The players stayed at a nearby Hilton, where they were given shoes and other Adidas gear when they checked in. In the lobby were agents, wanna-be agents, and representatives of agents. It was a breeding ground for corruption and unsavory characters looking to get their hooks into the next Michael Jordan or Kevin Garnett.

As for the games, most of them were offensive in style, with little passing and lots of shooting. They also were appalling to the eyes of coaches, who saw so little team basketball. James just took the ball, went right at Cooke, and usually overwhelmed the smaller guard. After watching James, Louisville coach Rick Pitino said: "There's a certain young man in there, that if he follows the path he is on, is going to be a star in the NBA. None of us should worry about recruiting him."

Pitino wasn't allowed to say his name due to NCAA rules.

One of the websites covering the event was prepstars.com, which wrote: "James makes it look too easy. So easy . . . The most common misconception about his game is his athleticism. Many fans who haven't seen him assume that he's some mind-blowing athlete with Vince Carter-like leaping ability. Not true. James certainly is a very good athlete, but it's his versatility and understanding of the game that sets him apart from others."

Actually, James was one of the most physically gifted athletes to ever play high school basketball anywhere, but because he was so smooth, so under control, it seemed like he didn't jump that high, run that fast, move from side-to-side that quick. He was so big—especially compared to the other high school kids. This was despite a roaring case of acne that was ravaging his 16-year-old face that summer, he seemed like a 10-year pro toying with everyone else. Sonny Vaccaro and most of the college scouts at that camp believed James would be a lottery pick at 17, after his junior season. James and his family did check out the early road to the NBA and discovered massive road-blocks. Under the labor agreement between the NBA and the NBA Players Association that ran through 2004, a player must meet several criteria to qualify for the NBA Draft.

First, his high school class must have graduated. James' class was scheduled to graduate June 7, 2003.

Second, a player must declare at least 45 days before draft day. That meant James' decision would have had to been made known by late April of his junior year.

In 1970, Spencer Haywood sued the NBA and won a legal victory under a violation of the Sherman Antitrust Act challenging a similar law. At that time, the NBA had a rule forbidding players from playing in the league until their college class graduated. Haywood played at the University of Detroit and wouldn't have been eligible to turn pro until 1971. That led to the creation of what was called the "hardship" draft rule in which a player could leave college early, claiming he and his family were under financial hardship. That ban was eliminated with the new players' collective bargaining agreement in 1976. Under that same principle, a player like James could try to win in court and enter the draft before his high school class graduates. But the NBA, which already has stated its concern about the growing number of high school players skipping college, would be vigorous in defending its rules in court. The result could be a long and expensive legal battle that could drag on past that April deadline.

In the end, James and his family realized this was not a battle worth fighting. Nor was it wise to quit school early just to play for pay in Europe, awaiting the NBA. It was to James' credit that as he considered his future, he not only decided against the lure of trying to be this generation's Spencer Haywood—he rejected chances to attend out-of-town prep schools such as Oak Hill, preferring to finish his high school career with Dru Joyce III, Willie McGee, Sian Cotton and Dru Joyce II, his summer league coach from his elementary school days who had replaced Dambrot as the head coach at St. Vincent-St. Mary.

So he waited one more year, and it was worth it to everyone from Nike to the Cavaliers to James.

CHAPTER 7

"THE CHOSEN ONE"

Courting LeBron

Just as the Cavaliers longed to get the right guy to lead them out of the basketball wilderness, so did the shoe companies. Yes, Michael Jordan was great. But by the summer of 2002, he was heading into his last season. No longer was he the king of the shoes. Others such as Vince Carter, Tracy McGrady and Kevin Garnett had failed to win championships and sell the volume of shoes that their companies hoped. None came close to grabbing as much of the market as Jordan.

Just as the NBA was looking for the next Jordan, so were the shoe companies. Getting the right guy meant mega-millions to them because of the business he'd bring to the company. They began to scout and recruit talent, just like college and pro teams. That's how men such as Sonny Vaccaro and the summer camps sponsored by shoe companies became so important to young stars like James.

Vaccaro is a legend in the amateur basketball world. After a career as a professional gambler bottomed out, the enterprising Vaccaro found a new career in a new business. Working as a promoter in Pittsburgh in the early 1960s, Vaccaro created the Dapper Dan Classic, which turned out to be the first national high school all-star game. He then pioneered the so-called "grassroots" movement in basketball. In his efforts to identify young basketball talent across the country, he found himself in a position to establish meaningful relationships and give advice to kids with huge hoops dreams—connecting them to shoe companies with dollar signs for hearts. Yes, Vaccaro helped bring attention and develop skills of hundreds of young gifted players, first through his all-star game and then through his annual ABCD summer instructional camp. But his real business turned out to be identifying potential stars for shoe companies. It was an enterprise that both enriched him and bonded him to some of the game's greatest players and operators. During his 40-year career, Vaccaro worked for three of the shoe giants: Nike, Reebok and Adidas. His most noted catches were Michael Jordan for Nike in 1984, and Kobe Bryant for Adidas in 1996.

Vaccaro bet his job on the success of Jordan, who Nike signed for $500,000 a year and a percentage of revenue from his signature sneakers. It was a revolutionary idea at the time, and Jordan, Nike and Vaccaro all won when Jordan became the biggest brand name in the history of athletic shoes. Companies such as Nike became corporate giants because of their affiliations with sports stars such as Jordan and Tiger Woods.

The Vaccaro legend was made by Jordan, then grew with Kobe Bryant. In 1995, three years after Vaccaro's bitter departure from Nike, one of his old Dapper Dan All-Stars named Joe Bryant brought his son to Vaccaro's ABCD Camp. Growing up in Italy, where his father played pro ball, Kobe Bryant was unknown in the U.S. basketball circles. Vaccaro helped him nurture his reputation and set up a relationship that led the preps-to-pros star to choose Adidas ahead of Nike. Just as Jordan's signing put Nike on the basketball map against powers Converse and Reebok, landing Bryant gave Adidas a big-time star to build around.

What few fans realized was that before James was being romanced by the shoe companies, he subtly began to recruit them with the help of family and friends.

It started in 1999 in a hotel suite in Tampa during the NCAA Final Four. Chris Dennis was an Akron summer league AAU coach who was close to the James family. He also had ties to California amateur basketball power brokers and some of the NBA's top agents. Dennis was in Tampa visiting with some of Adidas' executives. With NBA teams drafting high school stars and grassroots development bearing fruit and profits for shoe companies, entertaining and listening to summer league coaches had become standard business. Dennis told two of Adidas' point men—a San Francisco Bay Area AAU coach named Calvin Andrews and a summer league recruiter named Chris Rivers, who were friends of Vaccaro—about an amazing eighth grade basketball player from Akron. While it may seem unreal to think that shoe companies wanted to hear about a 14-year-old, that was exactly the process as the shoe companies and summer leagues and camps looked for the best young players. At this meeting not much happened, other than Dennis spreading the name of LeBron James. A year later at the 2000 NCAA Final Four in Indianapolis, Dennis saw them again in a hospitality suite. This time he brought a tape and a biography packet on James with newspaper articles and statistics. Andrews and Rivers took the tape, watched it, and then delivered it to Vaccaro. It was the first time Vaccaro saw or heard about James, who had just finished his freshman year at St. Vincent-St. Mary.

"When we saw him after his freshman year, we were very impressed and we thought if he just got a little bit bigger, he could be phenomenal," said Andrews, the AAU coach who later became an NBA agent representing high-profile players like Carmelo Anthony. "When we saw him when he was 16, he was bigger and stronger. He got everything he needed, he had exploded."

Dennis, Andrews and Rivers arranged for James to come to California again for Vaccaro to witness James for himself, against some of the top high school players from California.

"You have to understand, at the time this was very taboo, to have a 16-year-old come to play so a shoe company could see him," Andrews said. "Sonny wasn't even sure. He said he didn't want to waste time flying to Ohio to see him. We talked him into just flying up from L.A. [where Vaccaro lives]."

They settled on that gym at the University of San Francisco. Vaccaro took a seat by himself in the bleachers under a basket near the doors in the old gym. In the first game, James was just average. That's when another member of James' traveling party, St. Vincent-St. Mary coach Keith Dambrot, stepped in. Taking James into a hallway next to a trophy case with NCAA tournament ribbons and trophies and a bust of USF star Bill Russell, Dambrot made it very clear what sort of opportunity he might be wasting.

"He was all upset because his shorts were too big, they were bothering him," Dambrot said. "I just wanted to refocus him."

"Keith got into him real good, let him have it," Andrews remembered. "The next game, the dude was amazing. He was killing guys."

Between a series of James dunks and jumpers and a 75-foot bounce pass to a teammate for a lay-up, Vaccaro fell in love. By the end of the session he was calling old friends and business associates to tell them he'd discovered another megastar in the making.

"There are a couple of special days that I'll always remember," Vaccaro said. "Meeting Michael at a Tony Roma's restaurant in Santa Monica, the day Joe Bryant brought his son [Kobe Bryant] into the gym and introduced him to me—and the day I saw LeBron play in San Francisco."

James revealed enough that the Adidas executives contacted St. Vincent-St. Mary to offer an equipment deal to start a relationship with James in the summer of 2000. Vaccaro later called it the best $15,000 he'd ever spent.

That was especially true by James' junior year when he was discovered by *Sports Illustrated*. The magazine sent reporter Grant Wahl to Akron at the end of January, and he spent four or five days with James and his high school team. James was open and allowed Grant to go everywhere and have lots of access. They did the photo shoot at the high school gym on a Saturday morning. This was his first major photo shoot. They wanted a high-energy picture, but James was tired and didn't understand why the photographer wanted him to show energy, passion and lots of vivid facial expressions. They sent out one of the photographer's assistants to get him juice and food (he hadn't eaten) so he would perk up. He proved to be quite photogenic, and the magazine put him on the cover—a 17-year-old LeBron James holding a gold basketball behind his right ear, as if he were ready to throw it like a football. His left arm is out—almost like a stiff arm from a running back. His mouth is in a huge O, his brown eyes are wide, his head is in a green sweatband. Next to James wearing his green and white No. 23 high school uniform is the headline, "THE CHOSEN ONE."

The subhead reads: "High school junior LeBron James would be an NBA lottery pick right now."

Inside is a six-page story by Wahl under the headline: "Ohio High School Junior LeBron James Is So Good That He's Already Being Mentioned As The Heir To Air Jordan."

The article quotes Danny Ainge stating: "There are only four or five players in the NBA that I wouldn't trade to get LeBron right now."

Wahl wrote: "Not only does LeBron have the high-flying game, but he also has an Iversonian street cred that Jordan himself lacked."

Today, this doesn't sound that outrageous. A strong case can be made that James is on course to make a run at Jordan's legacy, if you are willing to remember that it took Jordan seven years to win his first title. And if you are willing to admit that Jordan entered the league at the age of 21, compared to James at 18. But this was published on February 18, 2002. James was a junior in high school. James was just a kid. He was receiving hundreds of fan letters each month. He stopped signing *Sports Illustrated* covers for adults when he discovered they were being sold on eBay for more than $200.

"I went to see LeBron play, and I knew he was destined for greatness," said Wayne Embry, the former Cavaliers general manager. "It was a game at Cleveland State. The other team tried to rough him up. It didn't bother LeBron at all. He had tremendous size and physical strength. He could get to the basket any time he wanted. I was impressed with how he passed the ball and worked with his teammates. He was not just trying to score all the time. He played a team game. His jump shot needed work, but that was it. I still remember that he barely shot in the first quarter, instead getting his teammates involved in the offense. He still ended up with 30-some points."

Embry was just an advisor to the Cavs when he watched James that day. He is a traditionalist who hates the idea of high school kids coming to the NBA. He wishes they all would go to college, believing most should stay four years, earn a degree, mature and then pursue the pros. He rarely raves about a player in high school. But James was unlike any other high school player he'd ever seen. "I knew that if somehow the Cavs could get that kid, it would change the course of the franchise," said Embry, thinking back to James' junior year in high school.

On that same February 18, 2002, when James truly went national thanks to *Sports Illustrated*, the Cavaliers lost 103-92 to Utah before an announced crowd of 12,773 at Gund Arena. There were fewer than 10,000 in the seats. Meanwhile, James and his high school team were consistently selling out the University of Akron's JAR Arena, putting more than 6,000 fans into a place that holds about 5,500. Here's what it was like at a typical LeBron James game. Fans would stomp and cheer, and that was just when James' team began a pregame lay-up drill. He'd sometimes heave the ball against the top of the backboard, then race for the rim, soaring, then catch the ball with his elbows, his head in the basketball clouds.

Wham!

He'd throw the ball *down* through the rim.

Wow!

Fans would scream, screech and dream of him one day in a Cavaliers uniform.

During games, James would glide up and down the court, his feet seeming to seldom even touch the court. His strides seemed twice as long as any other player. His biceps bigger than many players' legs. His shoulders wider than Lake Erie, his eyes sharper than an eagle's. As a veteran Akron area coach named Frank Lupica from Walsh High school said, "He's something that comes along once in a lifetime."

Romeo Travis transferred from a local Akron public high school to St. Vincent-St. Mary for his sophomore season, which also was the sophomore year for James, Dru Joyce III and Sian Cotton. While Travis has known James since they were both eight years old and playing Pee Wee football against each other, it wasn't until Travis became a teammate that he discovered something startling about James.

"He has a crazy left hand," said Travis. "He shoots the ball right-handed, so I always thought he was right-handed. But he writes with his left hand. He can drive to the basket and shoot with either hand. He can throw passes with either hand. If you watch him close, you realize part of the reason he's so hard to stop is he can get you from either side because he uses both hands like most people use one."

Being able to convert driving shots with either hand—and from either side of the basket—is an enormous advantage. Very few high school and college players can consistently make lay-ups with both hands. Pro coaches complain that too many of their players always drive right, or drive left. They just won't put in the work to be confident enough to make short shots with both hands. Favoring one hand and one side makes them easier to defend.

"LeBron is great physically, but he's even better mentally," said his former high school coach, Keith Dambrot. "When he was a freshman, he was 6-foot-2, 170 pounds. His vertical leap was only 24 inches. I didn't worry about that, because I knew he'd get bigger, stronger and jump higher. But here's the thing, if LeBron had stayed at that same size as he was when he was a freshman, he'd still be a Division I college player and probably play in the pros. His skill level in the ninth grade was phenomenal. His mental ability was phenomenal. He's just a basketball genius. We had some guys who couldn't remember where they were supposed to go on certain plays, but LeBron knew. He knew where everybody was supposed to be on every play! That's part of the reason he can throw those long, blind passes—looking one way, and finding an open guy in the opposite direction. He doesn't just see the whole court, he knows what's supposed to be happening. My biggest problem in practice with him was keeping him from getting bored. He'd catch on to the new plays right away. But we had to go over it and over it so the other players would get it."

Some players with these mental gifts are the sons of coaches or star players. They grow up in the gym watching practices. Instead of cartoons, there are game tapes on their TV sets as dad scouts opponents and critiques his own team. They learn about Xs and Os along with the ABC's. But James had none of those advantages. Yes, he was blessed to be hooked up with strong youth coaches such as Dru Joyce II, Lee Cotton and Frank Walker—but it's not like Georgetown coach John Thompson Jr. growing up in the same home as a former Georgetown coach named John Thompson Sr. Or former Cavalier star Mark Price being raised by Denny Price, a former assistant coach at Oklahoma and a head coach at some small colleges. James is just smart, and not just in his ability to learn things quickly and remember them for a long time. As a young player, he was smart enough to know that being physically dominant isn't enough, the mental game was just as crucial—and he could learn a lot from his coaches and older, talented players.

After James' sophomore season, *USA Today* named its All-USA boys basketball team for 2000–01.

The newspaper picked Dajuan Wagner as the Player of the Year. Joining him on the first team were Eddy Curry, Kwame Brown, Kevin Torbert and James. Wagner, Curry and Brown would all be first-round draft picks, as would James. The second team was Tyson Chandler, DeSagana Diop, T.J. Ford, Julian Hodge and David Harrison. Chandler, Diop and Ford also would eventually be first round picks.

Of those 10 names, three would one day be drafted by the Cavs: Wagner, Diop and James.

By his junior season, *USA Today* had proclaimed James the top high school player in the country, the story running under the headline: "Sky's The Limit For USA's Top Player."

As respected basketball author Dan Wetzel wrote for CBSSportsline. com in January of 2002: "There has never been a better high school basketball player since kids started turning pro before the prom. Not Kobe. Not Garnett. Not T-Mac . . . LeBron James is a walking lottery ticket waiting to be cashed."

Wetzel's story contained a list of all the high school-to-pro players from 1995–2001. The best were Kevin Garnett (1995), Kobe Bryant (1996) and Tracy McGrady (1997). Others included Darius Miles, Kwame Brown, Al Harrington, Jermaine O'Neal and Korleone Young. Some names fans would know, others are forgotten because they never played much and were cut within a few years.

Nothing is guaranteed. Wetzel's story also had a list of the Top 10 high school junior players for 2001–02. James naturally was No. 1. But here are the rest in order: Leon Powe, Travis Outlaw, Lodrick Stewart, Kendrick Perkins, Dion Harris, Charlie Villanueva, Richard McBride, Chris Taft and Rodrick Stewart. As James was wrapping up his third All-Star season in the summer of 2007, none of the others on the list had even approached his accomplishments. Leon Powe and Kendrick Perkins were averaging fewer than five points per game for Boston. Chris Taft was on the end of the Golden State bench. Travis Outlaw averaged 10 points for Portland, and Charlie Villanueva was a solid starter and a 12-point scorer for Milwaukee. Four of the 10 were not even in the NBA.

While the Cavaliers had fewer than 2,000 season ticket holders, James' high school team sold more than 4,800 season tickets and usually packed the 5,500-seat JAR Arena on the campus of Akron University. James held formal press conferences after games as more than 20 print and electronic media reporters were at nearly every game. It was close to 100 for major opponents.

In the article, James told Wetzel, "Sometimes, it feels like I have the whole world on my shoulders. The whole city of Akron. I know I'm under the microscope in everything I do."

CHAPTER 8

"IT IS GOING TO COME DOWN TO MONEY"

The $hoe deal

King James wanted a triple crown . . .

To have his high school team ranked No. 1 in the nation by *USA Today*.

To be the first pick in the NBA draft.

To sign the biggest shoe contract ever given a rookie.

Yes, LeBron James wanted it all, and he played like it. Not only were his overall skills continuing to improve, he was performing under a massive media microscope against fierce competition. Playing a schedule against some of the nation's top-ranked high school teams, James and his St. Vincent-St. Mary team took down one after another. The games would be close for a while, then James would take over—driving to the basket, dunking on an overwhelmed opponent. He'd pass off to teammate Dru Joyce III for open 3-pointers. He'd find Romeo Travis under the basket, delivering passes leading to lay-ups. He threw in long jumpers and short, silky bank shots. NBA scouts watched him in awe, wondering how an 18-year-old with a man's body at 6-foot-8, 242 pounds could be so graceful, yet so powerful. The nation caught the LeBron James Show when ESPN2 broadcast two of his games, including a victory over previously undefeated Oak Hill Academy at the Cleveland State University Convocation Center. His St. Vincent-St. Mary Fighting Irish ended up winning it along with its third Ohio State Championship in four years. Then *USA Today* indeed named them the nation's top team. Remember that these were not a group of high school All-Americans recruited from across the country. They were mostly kids from Akron, none of them other than James even remotely regarded as a pro prospect. Only two of his teammates—Dru Joyce III and Romeo Travis—would play Division I college basketball. Both did for the University of Akron, and that's only because they were recruited by their former high school coach, Keith Dambrot, who had become an assistant at the school. Both also overachieved, starting for the school that became a Mid-American Conference power. But neither had anything close to a pro career. The reason St. Vincent-St. Mary had one of the greatest high school teams in recent memory was because they had one of the best high school players ever in James.

Off the court, there was controversy. James originally received a season-long suspension by the Ohio High School Athletic Association for violating amateur status rules when he took two throwback jerseys. James thought it was a fair exchange for giving the store some auto-graphed pictures. That probably was true as James memorabilia was bringing in big dollars on eBay and elsewhere. A high-profile lawsuit filed for James by one of Cleveland's top law firms convinced the court to cut the suspension to two games. The school hired personal security guards to protect James from the media and fans who wanted to reach him. Pros such as Shaquille O'Neal and Ron Harper—then with the Los Angeles Lakers—ventured the 60 miles from downtown Cleveland to Canton to watch James play a high school game. Attention was paid to the Hummer that James was driving, a gift from his mother. His stylish clothes and diamond earrings led to whispers, as it was obvious James was getting money from somewhere.

So how did James and his loose-knit family find a way to pay for these perks and trips to summer camps across the country? That's where Eddie Jackson came into the game. Jackson had an on-and-off relationship with Gloria James for several years, dating back even before James went to elementary school. If there was a father figure in the life of James, it was Jackson—as James would tell the media years later. Jackson played a larger role in both of their lives following the unexpected death of Gloria's 42-year-old mother Freda, when James was three years old. Jackson also helped the family during James' high school years.

When family friend Chris Dennis began to preach the gospel of sending James to different summer camps and having his family along to meet shoe company executives, Jackson knew he needed to find some money. His belief in the importance of James' gaining national exposure led to Jackson thinking very big—and he was not alone. Seeing the people already struggling to get the attention of the 16-year-old James and the travel and expenses it would require, Jackson decided to find financing for what appeared a whirlwind two years. He had already been helping to support the family financially for several years. Jackson began a process to help the family cash in on some of James' future equity. According to court records, Jackson used a friend to meet with an Akron-based entertainment agent, Joe Marsh, who was known for managing magician David Copperfield. Marsh met with Jackson and the family. In exchange for the promise of doing future business, including the rights to a potential documentary with James, Marsh agreed to give Jackson a $100,000 loan. He wrote out the first installment, a $30,000 check, just days after James returned from the ABCD camp in New Jersey in the summer of 2001.

Later, Marsh gave a $20,000 check to Jackson and $2,500 monthly installments to Gloria James, according to court records. Marsh believed the money was used to buy James and his mother new cars and to improve their living conditions on Akron's west side. The family also took out an insurance policy on James and his future earnings. The reason these transactions became public was because Marsh, spurned by the family when he tried to make the documentary during James' senior year, sued for $15 million and entered all the documents into the court record. After a drawn-out process that took nearly two years, Marsh ended up just getting his money back, plus $22,000 in interest.

James was never penalized by the Ohio High School Athletic Association for this, because Marsh didn't file the lawsuit until James had turned pro. But two years after striking the deal with Marsh, James became the center of national headlines when the Ohio High School Athletic Association looked into a Hummer H2 sports utility vehicle Gloria legally purchased for him. Since his mother bought it—probably with help, as most banks and car dealers would give her a loan knowing that her son would soon be a millionaire pro—there seemed to be no violation.

Jackson also talked to agents hoping to represent James when he did turn pro. Instead of the agents making the calls to the prospect, it sometimes was Jackson who called them as he ramped up interest. Jackson focused on two of the NBA's power brokers: Aaron Goodwin and Bill Duffy. Former partners in Oakland but rivals by this time, both wholeheartedly pursued James, regularly attending his games and family functions such as dinners and informal gatherings to watch games and talk. Also in the bidding was mega-agent Arn Tellem, who represented Kobe Bryant and was close to Sonny Vaccaro—who had become a friend of the James family, in addition to trying to sell James on the merits of signing a shoe contract with Adidas.

There were whispers and eyebrows raised when Jackson seemed so prominent in these talks. In 1993, Jackson was arrested and sent to jail for selling cocaine. When he was released, he came back to help support the family. When James was in high school and traveling across the country, Jackson was involved in a federal mortgage fraud scheme. He and at least four associates were inflating the value of run-down homes through shell companies and selling them. Prosecutors said the three-year scam duped mortgage companies out of more than $500,000. One of the shell companies was part of the paperwork in the lawsuit with Marsh. Jackson was arrested in the summer of 2002 and later plead guilty to racketeering, money laundering and forgery charges and received three years in a federal prison. James was devastated by the news; he saw it as his father being sent away. When Jackson reported to federal prison during James' senior season at St. Vincent-St. Mary, the 18-year-old moved into Jackson's home in Akron and lived there until turning professional.

While Jackson's methods could be called into question, his ability to support James and fund his trips proved to be invaluable to the overall process. Yes, James' game and ability was the fuel, but Jackson and Vaccaro helped drive and steer the national publicity machine— adding to James' reputation and value in the eyes of the shoe companies. During one memorable stretch in the summer of 2002 after he'd broken his wrist, James showed his shoe free agent status by going to both the ABCD Camp in New Jersey and Nike's version, the All-American Camp in Indianapolis. He couldn't play because of the injury, but still held press conferences. At the Nike event, he wore Adidas shoes.

At the Adidas event, he wore Nikes. The message was clear. He wasn't committed to anyone, and the shoe companies better be ready to battle for him. Family and friends were with him for the entire excursion and were in first-class accommodations. Jackson helped make it possible for James to get to big events, and even to see a specialist in Chicago several times after he broke his wrist in that summer game in 2002. Being at all the top-level tournaments and camps kept James in the headlines and kept his stock rising. Having his family and friends there with him helped his comfort level.

"Everything Eddie did to get LeBron ready was brilliant," said Goodwin, the agent who eventually won James' services and negotiated his first endorsement contracts. "In a way, I'm saddened that he hasn't gotten more credit for it."

In the language of the street and the men and women who operate on the grassroots basketball level, there are many like Jackson who have been a part of the rise of young athletes. Their tactics are questioned by those who don't know the inside game, but appreciated by many basketball insiders who understand that this is a game in which there are few clear rules.

"Eddie and Gloria did what they had to do, they played the roles they needed to play," said Chris Rivers, the Adidas grassroots coordinator who has gone on to become the director of basketball marketing at Reebok. "All of us—LeBron, Eddie, Gloria, Sonny, the other shoe people, the media—we all live in a gray area."

There was nothing gray about the final round of shoe talks during the spring of 2003 as the NBA draft approached. James seemed destined to be the No. 1 pick in the NBA Draft in June of 2003. But what shoes would he wear, and how much would a company pay to make James into their latest commercial commodity?

Thanks to Sonny Vaccaro, Adidas was the first to lay claim to James. James was going to their camps and tournaments and usually wearing their shoes. In articles in *Sports Illustrated* and *ESPN The Magazine*, the photos had James dunking in Adidas models. He'd been the guest of their star pitchman, Kobe Bryant, at the 2002 All-Star Game in Philadelphia. He'd helped design uniforms that Adidas made for his high school team. Vaccaro had James and his mother, Gloria, as guests at his home in Calabasas, Calif. He'd been the James' guest in Akron. Chris Rivers, Vaccaro's top aide at the time, was practically living in Akron during James' senior season to be close to the James family.

But Nike was the giant of the industry, and they had been watching James just as closely for two years. With Michael Jordan finally retiring for the last time, the pressure on Nike to develop another hit signature star was growing. They hired Maverick Carter, three years older than James and a former high school teammate. He also was a cousin, and close to James. Now, he was working for Nike during James' senior year. Yes, Nike wanted him bad. Real bad. It showed in March of 2003, when a report by a Merrill Lynch analyst discussed how James' signing could affect Nike's stock price. It drew a harsh reaction from Adidas, Reebok and even James' personal attorney. But it showed, from Main Street to Wall Street, the James shoe deal had massive stakes.

James represented a perfect pitchman. Not only was he already well known to basketball fans thanks to the magazine covers and huge national television coverage, but his game itself was easy to market. He had his highlight dunks, but he also proved to be an unselfish player who enjoyed sharing the ball. Aside from the hoopla over perks such as the Hummer bought for him by his mother, there were no negative stories about James' character. He wasn't in trouble with the law. He was a solid-B student at one of the best private high schools in Northeast Ohio. He was respectful to teachers and coaches, usually very polite in public. He had watched tapes of Jordan and others give press conferences and modeled himself after these media savvy stars as he was amazingly patient and mature dealing with the mass of reporters attending every game. Nike saw him as another Michael Jordan, another Tiger Woods. He could be a minority athlete whom the majority of fans loved because his personality transcended race. His game attracted both pure and casual fans. Nike had sent several members of its organization to court James, but none more influential than Lynn Merritt, the senior director of global basketball. Merritt on the front line was not Nike's traditional strategy. It revealed how serious Nike was about landing James.

Near the climax of the talks, it became obvious to the various companies that all the time spent building a relationship with James and his family was not the bottom line. It would come down to cash. Lots and lots of cash. During his senior year, James seemed to be toying with all the companies. James was wearing Nikes and Adidas shoes at games. He once even sported a pair of Reeboks that were shipped to him. It was a firm signal Reebok would be a player in this game, and James was declaring his shoe free agency, willing to listen to anyone. Before one game, Eddie Jackson was seated in the first row of bleachers at the University of Akron's Rhodes Arena, where James played his home games his last two years of high school. Dressed head to toe in shoe company gear of varying logos, Jackson casually chatted with a reporter about the impending shoe war.

"All the shoe people have treated us very nicely, they're great," Jackson said. "But it is going to come down to money."

That was what Vaccaro feared. When he convinced Michael Jordan to pick Nike ahead of Adidas, the offers were about the same. But Jordan and especially his father were sold on Nike's vision. When Vaccaro landed Kobe Bryant for Adidas, it was because Vaccaro had become a trusted advisor and friend. Vaccaro had a dream for James and had become a family friend, but it was fast becoming apparent that it wouldn't matter. That crystallized during a game in Los Angeles at UCLA in January 2003 where James' high school played in a tournament. Along one baseline sat Nike co-founder and CEO Phil Knight. Next to him was Howard White, a Nike vice president who ran the Jordan brand. Along the other baseline sat Vaccaro and Rivers. The shoe movers and shakers stared at each other the whole night as James bounced back and forth between them.

After not speaking to Knight in 10 years since the bitter breakup at Nike, Vaccaro walked over to him as he left the arena and whispered in his ear: "Be ready to fight."

It wasn't just business, it was personal, too.

"Deep down I always knew Nike would get him, because Phil could write the biggest check," Vaccaro said. "But I thought we had a chance."

In late April of 2003, James officially announced he was going to turn pro with a press conference at his high school. After listening to the pitches of several agents, he chose Aaron Goodwin partly because Goodwin had a history of making major shoe deals with various companies. Goodwin had sent Gary Payton and Jason Kidd to Nike . . . and the likes of Shawn Kemp and tennis stars Venus and Serena Williams to Reebok. Goodwin hired Fred Schreyer, a Portland, Oregon–based attorney who had been Nike's director of sports marketing for six years, to help in the negotiations.

Now the commissioner of the Professional Bowlers Association, Schreyer was at home in this battlefield—not only because of his history with endorsement contracts at Nike but because he personally knew many of the parties involved. So did Goodwin, who had a track record of landing huge deals for his clients. Goodwin and Schreyer being involved hinted that Nike was the favorite, considering Goodwin had done most of his basketball deals with them and Schreyer's background with the company. It is a stigma Goodwin fights to this day.

"I represent clients, not shoe companies," Goodwin said.

Still, Schreyer admitted Nike was always the favorite, partly because Nike usually pays the most.

"If Nike is behind you, if they are going to make the investment in you, that's the place you are going to go," he said. "Their track record with marketing marquee athletes and establishing icons is unparalleled. If you could get the best deal with Nike, all things being equal, you go with Nike."

In the weeks leading up to the official talks, which started in early May, Vaccaro had been doing his best to control expectations. The only shoe company representative granting interviews, Vaccaro repeatedly said James would likely get around $5 million per season for five years. That $25 million deal would have been a record deal for any player coming into the NBA, much less one straight from high school.

"Based on past history that sounded like a deal that was pretty good," Schreyer said. "Sonny was a pretty smart guy, he was trying to limit the marketplace. Value in that world is very subjective. It is driven by the market, it's what people are willing to pay."

One of Goodwin's first moves was to reach out to Reebok. He knew Nike and Adidas would come with offers, but he wanted to get as many companies involved in the bidding as possible. While they had been on the sidelines when it came to making inroads with James and his family, Reebok had a significant interest. Reebok developed much lower profile relationships with the James family, even sending Jackson letters at the federal prison where he was sent midway through James' senior season. Still, it was a challenge to make Reebok believe it had a legitimate shot at landing James. It seemed that their offer would be used as something to inspire Nike and Adidas to raise their bids. Goodwin told Reebok that they had a lot of ground to make up, but that James would give them an honest shot. It just had to be a strong shot, an earth-shaking cannon shot, the kind never heard before in the shoe wars.

With Reebok interested, a charged environment had been created. The three biggest companies were all ready to fight with their checkbooks and James was set to reap the reward.

"It was the perfect storm," said Darren Rovell, who covered the James shoe chase for ESPN.com. "It was also the most public endorsement negotiation in the history of sports, which not only changed how everyone perceived the deal but also the stakes for getting it done."

Goodwin shrewdly scheduled three visits to the shoe companies over the course of a 10-day period. He wanted Reebok to go first, then Adidas and, finally, the one with the most money, Nike. Having told Reebok to come strong with an offer, he was hoping they'd set the market and Adidas and Nike would raise the stakes.

On a Thursday afternoon after school, James, Gloria and Goodwin boarded a private jet and flew to Reebok's headquarters outside Boston. The presentation wasn't all that flashy, especially compared with what they'd see in the next two stops. James was shown sketches and mock-ups of potential signature shoes. But Reebok's pitch wasn't about flash, it was about cash. In a move that no doubt upset rivals at both Adidas and Nike, Reebok changed the game by unveiling a massive offer. Privately, Goodwin thought talks would start about the $30 million mark. He had prepared James to reject such an offer while getting the bidding game going. But even Goodwin was stunned by the first proposal put on the table. Reebok said they would give James $60 million in guaranteed money—and incentives that could raise the deal's value to around $100 million based upon sales and other factors.

Now that was a real shot, a shocking, unprecedented number for an 18-year-old who had yet to dribble a ball as a pro. Consider that Tiger Woods had the previous richest amateur-to-pro in history shoe deal—$40 million. His last contract was $100 million with Nike, and it came after winning several major golf tournaments when he was established as an unquestioned superstar.

Reebok really grabbed the family's attention when CEO Paul Fireman pulled out a $10 million cashier's check made out to James. If he signed that night, he could take it with him. Reebok said it was a one-time offer, take it or leave it.

"It was a preemptive strike because they felt it was their best chance to sign him and it was smart because it almost worked," Schreyer said. "Someone puts a big check in front of you, life-changing money, and threatens to pull it away. It is tough to walk away from that. But we had to figure the offers weren't going to get worse."

Goodwin had to do some convincing, but the James family left the money on the table, got back on the jet and headed back to Akron.

The next afternoon, a Friday, there was another private jet waiting for James to whisk him and several of his friends to Los Angeles for a weekend pitch from Adidas. They stayed at a posh Santa Monica hotel, attended a Lakers-Spurs playoff game and then spent a Saturday afternoon at a ocean-side mansion Adidas rented in Malibu. There were shoe models and logos along with a video presentation designed to entice James. The possible marketing campaign was outlined.

At the same moment, Adidas began a billboard campaign in Akron. The company rented signs and plastered the sides of city buses with messages such as DO YOU WANT TO BE THE NEXT SUPERSTAR? specifically targeted to James. Yes, Adidas was recruiting James on the streets of his home town by renting billboards to be seen by anyone driving around or taking a walk. It was like a 50-foot love letter to be seen by James, and everyone else in his city.

The Adidas pitch that day in southern California was at least two years in the making, and it was impressive. But word of the Reebok offer had reached Vaccaro and Rivers. It deflated them. They knew what they could offer. Unlike Reebok—which had its top executives doing the talking—things had to be signed off by the Adidas brass back in Europe. Raising the offer and wiping out Reebok wasn't likely. Goodwin said the Adidas offer was very large, around $121 million.

But it actually included far less guaranteed and upfront money than the Reebok deal. The Reebok offer in Boston two days before had effectively buried Adidas under a pile of dollar signs and decimal points. It was such a record-smashing package that it made Nike gulp after leaving Adidas gasping for air.

"Sonny was embarrassed by the offer," Goodwin said. "He wasn't getting backed up like he thought he was."

Vaccaro asked for more time to come back with a counter offer, but he knew his chance to snare James had slipped by. He believed it would happen in a tough fight with Nike. He was ambushed by the quick offer from Reebok that nullified all the groundwork he'd put in with James. Within a few days, Vaccaro called Goodwin and told him Adidas was out of the running.

"When I took LeBron to the plane, it felt like it was going to be the last time I saw him," Rivers said. "Sonny was responsible for him getting the offers he got, but I think we all knew it was a long shot for us."

Finally, it was Nike's turn.

James and his team made another cross-country flight on another luxury private jet, this time to Oregon and the Nike headquarters in the Portland suburb of Beaverton. It is a wondrous place, a campus that resembles a 1960s-era think tank with its rolling grounds, and people scurrying about dressed in everything from suits to lacrosse gear to jogging clothes. A circular drive wraps around lakes and playing fields set up for various sports. There are sleek buildings of glass and steel with present and past Nike endorsers' names on them: Bo Jackson, Mia Hamm, Tiger Woods, John McEnroe and more.

The arrival made an impression. So did Nike's presentation, which surpassed anything James had witnessed. After a greeting and pitch from Nike boss Knight, the party was taken down to the workshop where Nike designers had already made several examples of what would be his signature shoes. One featured a likeness of his treasured Hummer and others reflected his "King James" nickname. Then models emerged wearing different pieces of apparel Nike planned to market with James' name on them. He was made to feel like his hero, Michael Jordan. He was shown another video presentation with his highlights splashed into a potential campaign. Then four rappers emerged with lyrics written especially for James, which appealed to his love of hip-hop music.

But the dollars didn't match the show.

When it came time to talk numbers later on with the lawyers, Nike's offer came in below what Goodwin had expected. He said the initial offer was around $56 million in guaranteed dollars. Though Schreyer said they didn't reveal the Reebok offer, James' agents were sure Nike had heard all about it. The James camp was disappointed in the proposal.

"The presentation was impressive, they'd done a tremendous amount of work," Schreyer said. "Part of the thing you conclude from that is, you've seen how much they've put into this, they're not just going to walk away over a few million a year. They spent a few million to put the presentation together."

That's right, "a few million" just for the show to entice James. It made those Akron billboards from Adidas look like 25-cent postcards.

Goodwin's parting shot to Nike was to the point: "I was pretty clear. I said, 'If you want this kid, then show it.'"

Goodwin and Schreyer made a counter offer, laying out what Nike had to do to secure James. Perhaps Nike should've agreed then, because the war wasn't close to over. The price was rising by the day. The shoe companies were discovering that James and his business team were even tougher to beat in this arena than he was on the court.

Goodwin set a firm deadline to get the shoe deal done by May 21, 2003.

The reason was simple. May 22 was the NBA Draft Lottery or, as it would become known, the LeBron Lottery. With major markets like New York, Los Angeles and Chicago on the board with small markets like Memphis, Milwaukee and even Cleveland, Goodwin didn't want the location where James would play to impact the deal. James would be worth more to a shoe company in a mega-market such as New York or Chicago than he would in Memphis or Milwaukee. At least, that was the conventional thinking. But Goodwin wanted the deal done before the lottery. All those NBA franchises could wait for the ping-pong balls and luck to determine their destiny, but he was not about to bet on this lottery. He wanted a sure thing.

Continued talks saw Reebok increase its offer while Nike seemed reluctant to match. One reason may have been Goodwin and Schreyer were dealing directly with Reebok's top decision-makers in Paul Fireman and Tom Shine, Reebok's vice president. Reebok had made it clear they were willing to increase the ante at each stage.

Nike was allowing its lawyers to do the talking, which was standard practice. But this deal was anything but business as usual.

"The price escalated so fast, I don't think Nike knew what to believe," Schreyer said. "Reebok came so strong. If you're Nike, it wasn't a matter of being cheap. They played a dangerous game, but they had to test how willing LeBron was to go to Reebok. The price they ultimately paid was beyond anything they'd paid before. That's not something you do lightly."

A few days before the deadline, the Reebok offer was significantly better. Goodwin informed James it appeared that was the way it was headed. That news didn't stay private. On May 20, 2003, the *Akron Beacon Journal* reported Reebok had become the leader for James with an offer in excess of $75 million. The reaction from basketball and shoe people was shock, the deal was never expected to go so high. It did nothing but increase the pressure on Nike as talk shows and industry observers bantered about how Nike may be outbid by a top rival. Nike's history had been to play to win. When the company really wanted someone, it got him.

Goodwin said Nike was "several million per year" below Reebok's offer. Officials in Beaverton were issuing "take it or leave it" statements. On May 20, Schreyer and Goodwin made a final proposal to Nike via fax. Then Schreyer flew from Portland and Goodwin flew from Oakland to St. Louis. They met and traveled on to Akron and the Radisson Hotel in downtown to be with James and complete the deal—with someone. The morning and afternoon of May 21 passed with no word from Nike. Meanwhile, Fireman and several Reebok lawyers flew in from Boston expecting to make a historic deal for the company. When the Reebok executives arrived, James was already at the hotel. He had inked a deal with trading card manufacturer Upper Deck to sign 6,000 pieces of memorabilia per year. It included a $1 million signing bonus, James' first big paycheck.

James greeted the Reebok officials at the hotel. He then went to St. Vincent-St. Mary, which was just a few blocks away, to play some basketball. The idea was to keep him out of the room, but not too far away for when his signature was needed. After all the games, secret and public, all the talk of money, all those trips on commercial jets and private—the time had come to make the biggest deal in the history of shoes.

What happened next, though, is a matter of much conjecture. The details from the various sides conflict, and the emotions of some were still raw about it, years later.

"The only one who knows in his heart of hearts is [Goodwin]," said Rivers, who left Adidas with Vaccaro and is now at Reebok. "A lot of lives would've been different had things gone differently in that room."

Goodwin said that when the Reebok lawyers presented the paperwork for the contract, Schreyer found some differences in terms that had been already negotiated in the days before. When Goodwin brought it up, he said Fireman told him: "My sources tell me you don't have the other deals you say you have."

It seemed to be a partial truth. Adidas was out of the running and Nike hadn't matched Reebok's latest offer.

"Someone gave you some bad info," Goodwin said he told Fireman, and then he asked for a break.

Goodwin said within minutes of leaving the suite his phone rang. It was a call from Nike. But this time it was from Howard White, one of Phil Knight's confidants. He said Knight—not the Nike lawyers—wanted James. Knight wanted to get the deal done. With Knight more directly involved, the game changed very quickly. Within minutes, Goodwin said, Nike had upped the offer to near what Reebok had put on the table. Within a few more minutes, a fax outlining the pact was sent to the hotel. James was summoned to sign it as the Reebok executives waited in a suite to continue talks. The deal changed in 25 minutes, according to Goodwin's brother and partner, Eric. He was talking with Nike officials from the Goodwins' Seattle office. James signed the offer sheet and it was faxed to Oregon.

Goodwin went back to the Reebok officials and told them the talks were off, that James had gone in a different direction. Needless to say, there were some hard feelings because Reebok claims it would've been willing to adjust the terms, but never got the chance. Other people have other versions of a complicated story like this. There was a feeling that Reebok had been left at the altar after shaming Nike into delivering the final deal.

The bottom line was $90 million over seven years plus incentives, along with that original $10 million signing bonus that Reebok had first put on the table in front of James. It added up to $100 million. Shocked and furious, Reebok made some efforts to reach Gloria James at her home and on her cell phone. When she picked up the phone and saw who the caller was, she didn't answer. James may or may not have left money on the table, but he joined the company he seemed to like the best. That may have been the key. Goodwin knew James preferred Nike, and a wise agent will then try to make the best deal that matches his client's wishes. Nike is Jordan's company. While James was one of the most mature 18-year-olds anyone would ever meet—he still was a kid with Michael Jordan posters on his wall. As a kid, he sometimes had Jordan shoes on his feet.

"It's special to be a part of the Nike family, it is something I dreamed about," James said. "They welcomed me and my family. It was a decision I felt comfortable with."

Yes, James' representatives did what their client wanted and did it on their own schedule. They had billion dollar companies sweating and sometimes swearing as they chased an 18-year-old kid from the inner city of Akron. The result was a record-smashing number, a day before anybody knew what city he'd play in—and months before he'd play in his first NBA game. Those factors alone made the contract go down in history. It only upped James' growing national reputation and media outlets made it the top news story the next day, not just the top sports story.

"When you're signing a deal like that, it's a career deal, LeBron is not going to change horses midstream," Schreyer said. "Nike wasn't going to get him for 50 cents on the dollar, but it wasn't all about money . . . there are different ways to value deals."

After leaving the Radisson in a rage, Reebok officials released a statement the next day. Afraid of a hit to their stock after it was learned they'd missed out on James, it read in part: "While we believe LeBron James would have been a tremendous asset to Reebok, the costs associated with securing a long-term partnership with him was far beyond what we are willing to invest. Reebok's largest competitor simply put more money on the table and in the final hour—after carefully considering what is in the best interest of our business and our shareholders—Reebok elected to not match this offer."

This, too, was unprecedented. A company having to make such a public comment over an endorsement deal that never happened. Not a merger, not a takeover, but an endorsement deal.

"It was a unique sets of circumstances and we were able to drive an incredible deal," Schreyer said. "There was a sense with LeBron that he was the must-have guy of the moment. That coupled with several companies bidding allowed us to get a deal that was unprecedented. Everything was lined up. You had the guy, the goods, the interest. It was a function of the marketplace."

Yes, Nike got their guy . . . and James got about $100 million.

It turned out to be a great deal for both sides.

CHAPTER 9

"I KNEW WHY WE WERE DOING IT, BUT I STILL HATED IT"

Hitting bottom

No general manager of any major pro sports team had a job quite like the one now facing Jim Paxson. Since taking over as Cavaliers GM in the summer of 1999, his job was to dump long-term contracts, try to pick up aging veterans near the end of their own contracts—and find some young players who could one day become viable in the NBA. He inherited a team that was 22-28 in the lockout season of 1998–99, and finished the season losing 11-of-12. After six seasons, it was obvious that veteran coach Mike Fratello and the players had grown weary of each other. This is a league where the average coach survives fewer than three years with the same team, so Fratello did well to be around for six. It's believed the Cavaliers lost about $10 million in that 1998–99 season. The losses began to pile up every season after that as the attendance kept sinking. The average was 20,338 in 1994–95, their first season at the new downtown Cleveland Arena, then known as Gund Arena. By the 1998–99 season, it was 14,120. In the next four years—all before LeBron James—the highest average was 15,873. Those figures seem inflated because often there were fewer than 10,000 people in the stands.

"When I was hired during Shawn Kemp's last season [2001-02], one of the first meetings that I attended was how we could give away tickets and make sure people actually came to the games," said Tad Carper, senior vice president of communications for the Cavs. "Some of the games, there were fewer than 3,000 people there. We'd often announce an attendance of 12,000—we'd distributed that many tickets—but only 7,000 showed up."

They donated blocks of tickets to school and youth groups, which created a "mall" effect with teenagers not in the stands—they would keep walking around the arena concourse, talking on cell phones, talking to each other, having no idea who the Cavs were playing, much less the score. If you were a teenager, the Gund was not a bad place to hook up with someone from another school, maybe collecting some phone numbers and e-mail addresses. As for what was happening on the court—they could have been giving away 1,000 deluxe plasma TVs—the kids never would have known.

In dollars, those gates were often about $200,000 a night. That sounds like a lot, until you compare it to the LeBron Era. On a bad game night, the team rakes in at least $1.2 million. Most nights, it's more. It could be as high as $2 million for a playoff game. Seldom do the Cavs have a no-show rate of more than 5 percent (about 1,000), compared to at least 40 percent during many of the games in the years leading up the LeBron Era. It was much worse than what the Cavs wanted the public to know.

"Selling a ticket is one thing, but you want that fan in the building," said Carper. "The fan brings energy the to game. The fan will probably buy food and drinks, and maybe a shirt and souvenirs."

There's nothing good about empty seats, and the Cavs had a sea of them before LeBron, as the seats were an ocean blue. The Cavs were 32-50 and 30-52 in two seasons (1999–2001) under Randy Wittman. John Lucas followed, and the record dropped to 29-53 in 2001–02. Because Zydrunas Ilgauskas was fighting his way through foot injuries, these Cavs had only one player worthy of any attention. That was point guard Andre Miller. He was above average at everything from scoring to passing to defense. He was not The Guy, the one who can turn a franchise around. But he was good enough to keep the team from being terrible, and he had enough character so that he wouldn't quit. In the summer of 2002, the Cavs talked a lot about Miller as the guard from Utah was one year away from free agency. They also talked about the big picture. They talked about getting The Guy. They talked about how that meant you had to lose a lot of games. They talked about hitting bottom, and they talked about money. The team continued to lose about $10 million annually for the fourth year. By 2002, the season ticket base was under 2,000.

Somehow, the Cavs had to get The Guy . . . especially the guy from Akron.

"I sensed Gordon and everyone were just trying to hold on until we could get it turned around," said Carper. "I didn't know how we'd do it, but I always sensed we would. We had a lot of good people working very hard."

But here's the problem—working hard wasn't enough. Making some trades wasn't enough. Certainly cutting payroll wasn't enough. The Cavs weren't just a bad team, they were a bad team with little hope of getting better. From October 1994, when they moved from the Richfield Coliseum to downtown Cleveland, the team never won more than a single playoff game in any given season. It was like watching the same season over and over, the Cavs winning a few more games than they lost—clawing into the playoffs—then being rudely kicked out. While the Kemp trade stirred some interest for a season, the team never had anyone who gave the fans a reason to believe. They were caught in the middle—too good to draft high, but not good enough to make a playoff run.

In the late 1990s, the Indians dominated Major League Baseball's Central Division and twice went to the World Series. They had a star-packed lineup and they were the favorite sons of the local sports fans. The Cavs were just . . . well . . . there. Their attendance would have been worse, but the Browns had moved out of town and there was no football from the end of the 1995 season until the fall of 1999.

By the summer of 2002, General Manager Jim Paxson knew something had to give. He was very aware of LeBron James being a year away from the NBA draft. He also liked Carmelo Anthony, who had enrolled at Syracuse and most scouts assumed that for him college would simply be a one-year finishing school. The Cavs finished the 2001–02 season with a 29-53 record. As Carper said, from a public relations standpoint, it was even worse. Other than a small hardcore group, fans had stopped complaining about the Cavaliers. They didn't care. Even if the team would somehow climb back to .500 and slip into the playoffs, it was doubtful that it would cause much of a stir. In the Cavs offices, no one wanted to talk about it, but nearly everyone was thinking, hoping, praying—somehow, this team needed LeBron James, or at least a young star such as Anthony.

Paxson said that in June of 2002, the agent for Andre Miller approached the team about a new contract for the point guard. He said Miller was one year away from free agency, and unless he received a "maximum deal," he would walk away in the summer of 2003. Paxson didn't want to commit $84 million over six years to Miller, because he knew that Miller was not about to change the course of the franchise. He would be paid like a superstar, but not be a superstar. He also would chew up some cap room that they needed to make other moves for players.

Not long after Miller's demand, Paxson met with Bob Whitsitt, the general manager of Portland and Paxson's old boss.

"Trade me Andre Miller," he told Paxson. "Give me your No. 1 pick. I'll give you a bunch of guys with contracts in their last year, and you can have all kinds of salary cap room next summer. You can pitch it as a 'going for LeBron' kind of trade."

In other words, getting really, really, truly terrible to maybe get good.

Paxson then had a meeting with team legal counsel Dick Watson and owner Gordon Gund. He talked about Whitsitt's proposal. He said he didn't like the idea of trading a No. 1 pick, but he was open to moving Miller.

"The best thing is for us to take a step back, trade Miller for a younger player," Paxson said. He explained that Miller was "just good enough" so the Cavs would win "28-to-30 games" and that could be too many to get a high spot in the draft lottery. Then, he'd probably leave the team as a free agent, the Cavs having nothing to show for it. Miller averaged 16.5 points and led the league averaging 10.9 assists. He had trade value, even though he was a year away from free agency.

On draft day 2002, the Cavs were determined to trade Miller. Portland had little the Cavs wanted, but the Clippers seemed interested in Miller and were willing to part with the No. 8 pick and Lamar Odom. That trade was very close to coming off, but it had to be approved by Clippers owner Donald Sterling. NBA people know that Sterling is notorious for stalling, changing his mind, and it can be hard to figure out if he's serious. The Cavs had the No. 6 pick. Paxson really liked Caron

Butler, a forward who later became an All-Star. Coach John Lucas and several Cavs scouts preferred Dajuan Wagner at No. 6, a 6-foot-2 high-scoring freshman guard from Memphis State.

"My gut was to go with Butler, but I went with Wagner based on the other opinions," said Paxson.

He also thought he could trade Miller to the Clippers for the No. 8 pick and Lamar Odom, then use the No. 8 selection for Butler. They never could get Sterling and Clippers General Manager Elgin Baylor to agree to a trade. The Clippers then passed up Butler, who went No. 10 to Miami.

In the second round, Paxson made *the* selection of his time with the Cavs when he grabbed Duke power forward Carlos Boozer.

"I look back on it now and we could have come out of that draft with Wagner, Butler, Odom and Boozer," he said. "That would have really got us going in the a good direction."

That's true, but too good to get LeBron James in the 2003 draft.

"Here's the amazing thing," said Gund. "We nearly made a great trade for Miller that would have brought us Caron Butler. In the short term, that would have been good, but then we never would have gotten LeBron."

Because they would have won too many games, and Cavs fans would have moaned, "This team can't even lose when it wants to!"

A month after the draft, Paxson worked the deal that ensured his team would end up with James. He didn't know it. He was still bothered by his draft day trade falling apart. The Cavs finally traded Miller to the Clippers—a much different (and worse) deal. They picked up Darius Miles, the classic product of the AAU summer basketball system where the accent is on gifted athletes running and jumping and dunking. He's 6-foot-9, 210 pounds and his leaping nearly could match that of James. But he couldn't shoot, couldn't handle the ball and defense was a concept that not only had little interest, but was almost offensive to him. Based only on his athletic gifts—not any real basketball skill level—an 18-year-old Miles was the No. 3 pick in the 2000 draft. He went to the worst possible place, the Los Angeles Clippers. They have long been a dysfunctional organization with losing as constant as the traffic jams and smog over the Los Angeles freeways. It was the Devil's Island of the NBA. Coaches came and went. Players came and went. Fans seldom went at all. The Clippers played as if it were every man for himself—get me all the shots you can so I can get out of here!

"Darius had talent," said Paxson. "He was only 20, and I thought because of his quickness and athleticism, he would get better. He was not a bad kid, but he didn't have that winning motivation. He really didn't understand what it meant to be part of a team that is a winner. He was caught up like so many kids into what can I do to make my game look good, how many points do I score? How many shots do I get? How many rebounds? In the right situation, he could have been a better player."

The Clippers weren't that situation, and neither were the Cavs before James. Even in the right spot, you take a poor kid from East St. Louis at the age of 18 and hand him a contract worth about $10 million—as the Clippers did—and it's hard to tell him that he needed to improve in so many areas. That there was more to basketball than his terrific dunks and lively legs. If you wanted to lose, Miles was the kind of player to help you. So was Ricky Davis, a selfish gunner that Paxson picked up in October of 2001. While Davis did play much harder than Miles, he played purely for his own statistics. He also felt threatened by anyone else who wanted to score.

"We put Ricky Davis and Darius Miles on the cover of our [2002-03] media guide," said Carper. "We hyped them to media as some of the young players whom we'll be building on for the future. Then came media day, and neither one showed up. Darius said his alarm clock didn't go off . . . and Ricky was somewhere else, out of town."

The alarm clock excuse seemed lame, because the media session was in the middle of the afternoon. Word was that Davis was "delayed in Iowa." No one knew what that meant, although he lived there for a while.

"Things like that kept happening," said Carper. "Those guys were young. There really wasn't any message about winning. It seemed like we were on an incredible streak of bad luck."

The Cavs had another strange event that fall. Veteran Lamond Murray—another selfish shooter—wanted to be traded. Part of the reason was he could not find a Cavs jersey with his name on the back at the arena team shop—as if there were fans demanding to wear

Murray's shirt. Paxson shipped the 16-point scorer to Toronto for an end-of-the-bench veteran in Michael Stewart and a future first round and second round pick. That first-rounder was later traded for Sasha Pavlovic.

Paxson also shipped Wes Person to Memphis for Nick Anderson, who retired. Miller, Person and Murray were the team's top three scorers the season before. Now, their points and contracts were gone. He was saving ownership a lot of money, knowing he would look like an idiot for putting together such a weak team—at least in the short run. That was OK, because if ever a bad team needed bad luck and bad players, it was the 2002–03 Cavaliers. A lot had to come together to bring LeBron James to his hometown franchise.

Some of this would be funny, only something tragic happened in the middle of the season that few fans knew. On New Year's Eve, during the worst season of Paxson's basketball life, when he was running a team designed to lose . . . and just when he was convinced nothing else could go wrong . . . it did.

His wife, Candice, had been suffering from severe headaches for a while. Medicine didn't work. Rest didn't work. Nothing worked. On that New Year's Eve, December 31, 2002, Paxson realized his wife had a problem. A very serious problem. He didn't know how severe, but he was sure these weren't migraines. Something was very, very wrong.

"We had an MRI set up for that night at 7 o'clock," said Paxson. "We went in for the test, came home and we weren't in the house for 15 minutes when the phone rang. It was the doctor, and he said we had to come back in."

That is never a good sign. Nor was the look on the faces of the two doctors who met them. They had the MRI scans, and began talking about two tumors. One was "significant," one "not as significant." Both were in the brain.

Immediately, they both thought, "Brain cancer."

Candice Paxson broke down into tears. Her husband tried to comfort her, but his hands were shaking, his stomach churning.

Tumors in the brain? How could some as bright and beautiful and young as his wife have tumors in the brain? She was 53, looked and acted even younger.

"They just said it was a tumor," Paxson told her. "They didn't say it was cancer."

But how often do you hear of someone who has brain tumors, but no cancer. Yes, there are cases . . . but they seem to be exceptions.

"They brought her back to the hospital on January 2, 2003, and ran all these tests," said Paxson. "She didn't want to have a biopsy right away because it happened so fast. They put her on a steroid, and it did reduce the tumors. The tumors began to shrink, but when they weaned her off the steroid, they came right back. This was over a period of two months."

There was no doubt, it was cancer. The doctors didn't say how long Candice could live, and the Paxson didn't ask.

"It was so hard to believe," he said. "We had been married nine years. She never had been sick at all until April [2002] when she had a ruptured appendix. She nearly waited too long to go into the hospital. She thought she just had the flu. But a ruptured appendix can kill you. I asked the doctors if when you have a ruptured appendix and it dumps that poison into your system, can that lead to cancer? They said they didn't know."

Candice Paxson had always been a "strong person," according to her husband. She ran her own businesses, starting with a clothing store in Portland. That's what she was doing when they met. Later, she started a promotional company, and it was very successful. She sold the promotional business when struck by the cancer.

"So you take a very independent woman who is used to doing everything for herself, and suddenly she can't drive," said Paxson. "She began receiving these cancer treatments that just wipe you out. At one point, she went through 34 treatments where they ran a catheter up the femoral artery to the base of one of the arteries of the brain. They have this solution called manitol that breaks down the barrier by the brain, they put the chemo directly into the brain. It can affect your hearing. You are exhausted. She had to take a shot of a blood thinner after each treatment [so she wouldn't have a stroke]. She was on so many pills. After some of the treatments, she'd be on the couch for a couple of days, watching the food channel until she fell asleep. There was nothing else she could do."

And nothing Paxson could do.

"You think you're a strong person and you think you can deal with anything, but it humbles you to see someone you really love and care about go through that," said Paxson. "You don't know what's going to happen. You can't control anything. You just go through it."

Meanwhile, his team was losing night after night. He needed to scout, or at least makes sure he had scouts at key college and high school games because he had no idea where the Cavs would draft in 2003. He wanted the top pick, but the lottery system was designed to make sure that there were no sure things about the draft. His leadership was being attacked in the media because the team was going backwards on his watch—he couldn't tell them that was the plan. Yes, he could talk about building for the future, about gathering young players, about patience eventually paying off. But all fans and the media saw was a terrible team in a near-empty arena.

"What got me through was how Gordon Gund and the entire organization stayed behind me," said Paxson.

Being blind, Gund understood the pressures facing an executive in a high profile position with a very serious personal issue. He knew there were moments when Paxson would feel like he couldn't do anything right. His team was losing. Candice's treatments seemed to be going nowhere, other than making her even sicker. Losing hair. Losing hearing. Losing some of her sight. Losing appetite. Losing so much confidence. Trying not to lose hope.

"As much as I cared about doing the best job I could for the franchise, the job doesn't define who I am," said Paxson. "There were times when I had to put Candice first. On Thursday nights, I used to watch the NBA doubleheader on TNT. But that became our date night when she was feeling up to it. We'd go to a movie, to dinner, just something to get out of the house."

"A lot of GMs could never do what Jim did for us in the couple of seasons before we got LeBron," said Gund. "He took the losing. He did what was best for the franchise and for ownership. Most GMs are too worried about their records and their reputations to be willing to go through what Jim did. Rather than worry about what was best for his career, he put the team first. Then you see what he did when his wife was sick. He did an exceptional job."

Paxson said the type of cancer that his wife had usually means a life span of three-to-five years, but she continued to survive and beat the odds. Paxson spent a lot of time researching it on the Internet. He found some people who lived 12 or more years with it. Others died in nine months. (Candice Paxson eventually died in 2007, four years after being diagnosed with cancer.)

"I didn't sleep much that season," said Paxson. "I was glad I had the job, because doing something else helped me deal with Candice's illness. But what was happening with the team really bothered me. I hated the losing. I knew why we were doing it, but I still hated it."

This was Paxson's first general manager's job, and he knew that while he was putting the Cavs in position to succeed, he was not helping his own career. But that seemed like a minor concern compared to taking care of his wife.

If there were any doubts the Cavs played this season with one eye on LeBron James, consider that Coach John Lucas had both eyes on James in the summer of 2002. James joined some Cavs players and some other local college players and pros for a workout at Gund Arena, which Lucas happened to attend. So did a newspaper reporter, who wrote how James held his own against the pros. The NBA didn't like this. The NBA has rules against a high school junior working out with pros at an NBA arena in front of a pro coach. The Cavs were fined $150,000. Lucas was suspended for the first two games of the season.

Word of the workout spread, especially a play where James caught a pass on the baseline. He took one dribble. Then another dribble. Then he jumped. Then he soared. Then he seemed to rise just a little higher, right over a 6-foot-5 NBA veteran named Bryant Stith, and he slammed the ball through the rim. Mouths dropped. The backboard shook. Stith stared at James, not saying a word, just making a T with his hands—the NBA indication for a timeout. Then Stith walked off the court, shaking his head.

All of this was reported in the Cleveland *Plain Dealer*. It was enough for local fans to dream even deeper and longer of the day when James would be playing at Gund Arena, only wearing a Cavs jersey. For that to happen, the Cavs had to lose. Given that was the basic plan, they were a spectacular success in 2002–03. They weren't just bad. They were terrible. They were 1-1 in October, 1-15 in November, 4-10 in December, 4-11 in January . . . you get the idea. The final record was 17-65, the third worst in franchise history.

Ricky Davis was suspended by Lucas early in the season for two games because he screamed at several teammates. Davis would average 20 points that season, but had a remarkable ability of making most of his teammates worse—or at least angry at him because of his selfish play. He shot 41 percent. In a game where the Cavs were shocking everyone—including themselves—because they were leading Utah by 25 points, Davis needed a rebound for a triple-double. With six seconds left, Davis took the ball and shot it at his own basket. He then went for the rebound, but was body-checked by Utah's DeShawn Stevenson—denying Davis the 10th rebound and a triple-double. Davis became the poster-player for total selfishness, and a symbol of the dysfunction on the Cavs team that season. Darius Miles seemed distracted and floated through the year, wishing he were somewhere else. Dajuan Wagner hurt his knee and needed surgery. Zydrunas Ilgauskas was healthy, but the veteran big man looked in constant pain with all the chaos around him. He was offended by the players who would not share the ball, who would not even make a pretense of defense. The only good part of the season (besides losing and positioning themselves for LeBron James) was the emergence of second-rounder Carlos Boozer, who averaged nearly 10 points and 8 rebounds. When the season mercifully concluded, the 17-65 Cavs tied Denver for the worst record in the NBA—and set the stage for the LeBron Lottery in New Jersey.

CHAPTER 10

"THAT GUY SHOULD BE YOURS"

The LeBron lottery

The franchise-shaking moment occurred in a normally quiet and unassuming four-story beige building tucked into a faceless office park just off the New Jersey Turnpike. It was between a busy Wal-Mart and a Courtyard hotel, at the NBA Entertainment structure in Secaucus, N.J., that LeBron James became a Cavalier. For 364 days each year, the facility operates in relative anonymity. One night each year it comes alive with excitement during the NBA draft lottery. And on May 22, 2003, it was where the Cavaliers franchise was reborn. On that night at somewhere around 7 p.m. in conference room 3A, four ping-pong balls with the numbers 6, 2, 3, 12, bubbled up and delivered LeBron James to his hometown team.

That night was perhaps one of the most anticipated events in Cavs history.

There have been a handful of times when the draft lottery became a must-see event because the top player available was wildly coveted by the league. The two most memorable such occasions were in 1985 when Patrick Ewing was emerging from Georgetown, and in 1992 when Shaquille O'Neal was coming out of Louisiana State. It was known on the night of those draft lotteries that the winner was going to take the obvious grand prize.

James' big lottery night held equal intrigue, not just because most knew he'd be the draft's top pick for the year, but because he was the first high school senior to generate such buzz. If most basketball fans hadn't already seen James play or his highlights from national television games with St. Vincent-St. Mary, they certainly heard about him on lottery day. Just the night before, James struck a history-making deal with Nike for nearly $100 million over seven years. It was such a shocking figure, especially for an as yet unproven 18-year-old, that it led newscasts across the country. It was as if Nike was saying James would be the next Michael Jordan, the next Tiger Woods—and betting a fortune on being right. Even basketball people were stunned by the shoe contract, as most estimates and rumors had it in the $20 million range, certainly no more than $40 million. All that for an 18-year-old who'd never dribbled a basketball beyond the high school level.

The big shoe money just turned the burners up higher on the lottery hype. ABC had the rights to televise the lottery and knew the demand to find out James' destination was so strong, that for the first time the network decided to build an entire show around the lottery. Normally it was a swift affair shown during halftime of a playoff games, sometimes on a lazy Saturday afternoon. With LeBron James turning pro, business never was as usual from the moment he appeared on the *Sports Illustrated* cover as a high school junior. Everything was on fast forward. This lottery became the LeBron Lottery. It was a primetime television special before Game 3 of the Eastern Conference Finals between the New Jersey Nets and Detroit Pistons. Ironically, that game was taking place just two miles away across the North Jersey swamplands at Continental Airlines Arena. But it seemed a world away to many of the teams who came hoping for luck and a basketball savior.

To accommodate all the unusual visitors, the NBA set up a tent in the parking lot where a makeshift media room and dining room were installed. A soft rain fell as the players started arriving. Cavs owner Gordon Gund and his close business associate Warren Thaler made the hour drive up from Princeton, which sadly had become an annual ritual as the Cavs were in the lottery for the fifth straight year. This, however, was no routine night.

"I'm on the board of the Kellogg Company, and the day before the lottery, I flew to Battle Creek, Michigan, for a meeting," said Gund.

Because the Cavs owner is blind, his material is read by assistant on to tapes, which he plays at a faster than normal speaking speed—his ears and intellect are trained from years of doing this that he can literally listen fast. He had been hearing stories of James for a few years, as material about the Cavaliers is also read on the tapes prepared for him each day. But as he listened to tapes about Kellogg and the upcoming meeting, he was thinking about ping-pong balls. He was thinking about what James would mean to the franchise.

"I was dreaming about getting him," said Gund.

Gund kept telling himself what Jim Paxson had told him, "No matter what, we'll get a good player even if we don't get LeBron."

Paxson's top three were James, Carmelo Anthony and Dwyane Wade—in that order. He had Anthony a close No. 2 to James.

"It's possible if we had the third pick and Anthony and LeBron were gone, we might have considered trading it," said Paxson. "I liked Wade a lot, but I don't think anyone knew he'd become such a great player."

Paxson said he believed the draft would have James and Anthony as the first two picks, Darko Milicic being No. 3. Paxson had scouted Milicic in Europe and was totally underwhelmed. He projected the 7-footer as exactly what the Cavs didn't need—a project requiring patience and lots of work. After Wade, he had Chris Bosh and Kirk Hinrich, in that order.

"Bosh was intriguing, but he still had a thin frame and could probably have used another year in college," said Paxson. "Wade was a combo guard. Was he better as a point? Or a shooting guard? He was just a very good guard. The top player was LeBron."

Gund wanted to be sure that James was more than a local legend. More than once, he asked Paxson about James.

"That's because Jim was not from the market," said Gund. "He would not be swayed by public opinion. He could evaluate LeBron in a cold, hard-nosed manner. And he was convinced about LeBron being special, that it had nothing to do with LeBron being a hometown favorite. He would be a great player."

A great player from the Cavs backyard in Akron?

It really seemed too good to be true for a franchise where most of the breaks weren't just bad, they were compound fractures.

While Gund would be in New Jersey for the lottery—flying in after his Kellogg meeting—Paxson stayed home in Cleveland. His wife, Candice, was receiving cancer treatments. He took her to chemotherapy, and this was a brutal procedure where they "put the chemo directly into the spinal fluid of her brain . . . I'd sit and talk with her, then take her home. She was so tired when we got home that she had to rest. I went out and washed the car. I got some groceries. I was just trying to keep busy."

For obvious reasons, Paxson was telling himself that this was important, but not a matter of life and death. Every trip to the doctors since the tumors were discovered near his wife's brain certainly added context and priorities to his life. But he still was nervous, still wondering if for once, something really good could happen to his basketball team.

"I wasn't privy to the numbers, but I remember being told that we were bleeding [losing] $1.5 million per month," Paxson said. "It had been like that pretty much for a couple of years. Gordon was taking a real hit."

And Paxson knew that James would change all that.

"No way we could miss from a business perspective," he said. "And I had no doubts that he'd be a star."

In New Jersey, Gund was met by Cavs vice president of communications Tad Carper, who had flown in from Cleveland with a special item. It was a jersey in the Cavs' new wine-and-gold colors with James' name and No. 23 on it. The Cavs had gotten special permission from the league to bring it, just in case.

"Only four or five people even knew the jersey existed," said Carper. "I stuffed it in my bag. I just wanted it in case we finally got lucky."

In his suburban Cleveland home, Paxson was nervously eating the pizza his son and a friend had ordered for dinner.

"I can't begin to describe how nervous I was," Paxson said. "I was sitting there with Candice . . ."

Winning the lottery doesn't change cancer, but it sure can lift a mood. Candice knew how hard her husband had worked to improve the Cavs salary cap situation. She knew the struggles, the obstacles, the sleepless nights. She knew how he had been doing two jobs— helping her deal with the cancer and running the Cavaliers. For good reason, it often seemed like there were never enough hours in the day.

The Cavs had the best odds along with the Denver Nuggets of winning, but it was just 22.5 percent. Less than a one-in-four shot. The Cavs didn't want to get anyone's hopes too high.

According to NBA rules, they could pick no lower than fifth. But that would seem like a very disappointing consolation prize, especially as

James, Wade and Anthony would be gone. The Cavs tried not to think about that, for obvious reasons.

About 40 miles south in downtown Akron, James and dozens of family and friends arrived at the Radisson Hotel, where James had rented a suite to watch the lottery. The day before he showed up at the hotel to check on the shoe contract talks, which were going on there. He signed a contract his agent, Aaron Goodwin, had worked up with Upper Deck, a trading card company that wanted 6,000 signatures a year on items from James, that made him his first million. The deal had a seven-figure signing bonus and Goodwin handed him the check, which James folded and stuck in his pocket—then left to go play pickup basketball.

Just off the hotel's lobby in a conference room, cameras were being set up for a press conference James would hold after the lottery.

James wanted to share this moment with his family and teammates from St. Vincent-St. Mary. Not just a few, but ALL his teammates would be there in the luxury suite.

Back in New Jersey, there was plenty of tension in the tent as everyone waited for things to get underway. Gund asked reporters from Northeast Ohio who had traveled in for the lottery to have dinner with him. It is not often owners and reporters eat together, but this was no ordinary moment. The conversation was wandering yet tense. Although media members are supposed to be objective, there was little doubt that everyone at the table wanted to see James stay home— Gund for the franchise's sake and the writers' for the story's sake. Over the previous two seasons, two of the three newspapers that normally traveled on the road with the Cavs had stopped and area columnists and television stations had been devoting less time to the franchise as it languished.

About two hours before the lottery Gund was slowly munching on a cookie. He twirled a wine glass with his left hand as he spoke. He was wearing a red tie, matching the Cavs new colors, and hoping for good luck for once. The Cavs had never won the lottery.

Around 6:30 p.m., it was nearly time for the team representatives to be locked in a conference room for the actual lottery. The results were shared about an hour later live on air in the studio while the conference room remained on lockdown to assure surprise. Thaler, a

Princeton graduate who had become Gund's protégé and the president of his venture capital firm, had asked Gund if he could represent the team in the conference room. Gund, who wanted to be on stage for the huge announcement, agreed. Before they parted in a hallway outside the studio, Thaler could see his boss and mentor was visibly nervous and shaky about the gravity of what was about to take place. Thaler tried to reassure Gund that the results weren't all that important in the grand scheme of life.

"You know, Gordon, this isn't like finding the cure for blindness," Thaler said, referring to Gund's lifework to search for a cure for the disease that took his sight as a young man.

Gund froze and gave an answer that caught Thaler off guard.

"It's pretty damn close," Gund said.

The expansive studio was packed; seats inside had become a commodity. Some team officials and media couldn't even get in, others had to stand in the back and along the sides. Don Chaney, the New York Knicks coach at the time, had to squeeze in near the back.

On one side 13 seats were set up in two rows with each seat bearing a small podium with a basketball displaying each team's logo. Gund took the second seat in the middle. Next to a rotating glass globe was the main podium, where NBA Deputy Commissioner Russ Granik slowly tore open each large envelope to reveal the draft order. Opposite the assembled team reps were the TV hosts, led by Mike Tirico.

"I had not been on the stage for the lottery in years," said Gund. "But the NBA wanted me to be there. Besides, I was going anyway. I was talking to [Memphis general manager] Jerry West. He has always been lucky, so I felt good about that. I said to Jerry, 'Here we go again.' Jerry said, 'We wish you well, that guy [James] should be yours.' I had a lot to basketball people telling me that, and it was gratifying."

About 40 minutes before airtime, there was a rehearsal. Gund took his spot in the second seat. On his left was E. Stanley Kroenke, the self-made billionaire owner of the Denver Nuggets. He was dressed in a resplendent white suit and had brought with him a number of good luck charms sent in by Nugget fans. They didn't change the Nuggets' chances. With a matching 17-65 record, they had a 22.5 percent chance of winning, just like the Cavs.

On Gund's right was Toronto Raptors star Vince Carter. The year before the Houston Rockets sent star Steve Francis to represent them on stage in Secaucus and they defied the odds to move up and win the No. 1 pick, which turned into Yao Ming. Carter was the Raptors' attempt to follow the trend. Also on the stage that night were Antawn Jamison, who represented the Golden State Warriors, and Juan Dixon, who was representing the Washington Wizards.

Granik went though the envelopes, in the exact draft order. In the rehearsal, the Nuggets won.

Upstairs Thaler and the 12 other team representatives were stripped of all their cell phones and any other communication devices, and placed into lockdown. On the wall and on charts provided to each rep were 1,001 numeric combinations. Each team had a certain number assigned to them.

Over the years this process has been scrutinized by conspiracy theorists. But the NBA has had objective third parties run the proceedings and has even let media members in to observe the process, which only takes a matter of minutes.

So here was the moment. The balls were dropped into a clear sphere and it started spinning, just like on the nightly lottery show.

Thaler, usually a staid and composed man, felt his chest pounding. Tall and thin with sandy hair and wire-framed glasses, he fits the cliché of an Ivy League grad. Calculating and intelligent, Thaler had worked his way up to become one of Gund's most trusted advisors. He, too, was armed with a host of lucky charms. There was one of his daughter's favorite dolls, a blue tie he and his wife bought in Egypt, and others.

When the fourth ball was revealed, Thaler scanned the paperwork to see if the Cavs had the lucky number. Before he could confirm it, the lottery's winner was announced: the Cleveland Cavaliers. Thaler pumped his fist in singular excitement—everyone else in the room was either disappointed or disconnected. It was a moment captured on film and now hangs on the wall inside Gund's offices.

In the studio, the waiting was agonizing. The audience tensed as ABC went live on air. The hosts went through highlights and analysis as the players on stage shifted in their chairs. After a commercial, Granik started opening envelopes to reveal the draft order in reverse, from 13 to 1. The studio, despite its buzzing lights and rather large audience, was nearly silent. The sound of Granik breaking the crisp seal on each filled the room.

The first seven placards were in perfect order, as far as the Cavs were concerned. No surprises. That changed when Granik got to the Memphis Grizzlies, who were in the No. 6 spot with just a 6 percent chance of winning. They were skipped, revealing they'd jumped into the top three. Team president Jerry West, in the midst of a grand rebuilding project of his own, flashed a grin as the room buzzed for the first time. When Granik revealed the Miami Heat and Toronto Raptors as having picks five and four, the Cavs, Nuggets and Grizzlies remained as ABC headed to a break. At this moment, all three were winners. Their numbers came up, getting them into the top three.

As Thaler comfortably watched from the sealed room, the tension maxed out during the three-minute break. West moved next to Gund, who smiled and exchanged small talk with Kroenke, although they weren't truly wishing each other luck.

"Because of my blindness, I have light sensitivity," said Gund. "I don't just see dark. I see colors whirling, mostly white, when I'm exposed to a lot of intense light. That's why I keep my rooms dark. It's easier for my eyes. But on a TV stage like that with all the light, it was like a kaleidoscope. In fact, that kind of light increases the degeneration of my eyes, but I was not about to wear dark glasses on the set. I tried not to concentrate on all the specks of light floating around, or it would drive me crazy. It seemed like it took forever for those last three picks."

Back in Akron at the Radisson, James' hotel suite was pulsing as all considered the options. With big cities like New York, Chicago and Los Angeles out of the picture, staying home looked very attractive to James' friends and his family. Still, James wasn't sure.

"I went to a lot of those games the year before I was drafted and I saw how they played," James remembered thinking as the final three became clear. "It was home, but at first I wasn't really sure if I wanted to be a part of that team after what I'd seen."

The fans gathered across Northeast Ohio were sure it was the right move and were waiting to discharge plenty of years of frustration. So was the man sitting in the second chair in Secaucus. Granik eyed the director next to the camera, who gave him the signal to resume. He quickly revealed the third pick . . . the Nuggets. The Cavs had beaten the opponent with the same odds to win.

Which ushered in the moment all had been waiting for. The pressure was enormous. Gund was so close to landing the franchise-changing player he'd dared to dream about for months. West and the Grizzlies fans were facing an all or nothing situation. They had traded their pick to the Detroit Pistons six years earlier, for Otis Thorpe, and only got to keep it if they won the No. 1 pick. It was the crown jewel or the sidelines for Memphis.

"When Denver came up third, I was so emotional sitting there with Candice," said Paxson.

Could it really happen? Could the gamble of tearing down the team to build it up again with someone such as James really work? Would the Cavs actually beat those 22.5 percent odds?

As the enveloped opened, Granik pulled out the red and green logo of the Grizzlies, meaning they'd won the No. 2 pick. "Which means . . . " Granik started. Few heard him finish.

Within seconds of Granik opening the envelope, Carper had rushed on stage with the No. 23 jersey to deliver to Gund, who was fast on his feet and quickly shaking hands, posing for pictures and doing interviews.

"We had changed the colors back to the original concept of wine and gold," said Gund. "No one saw the new uniforms until that night. I held that jersey and kept thinking what a great night it was for all the people in Northeast Ohio. This franchise finally got some luck. That was the first thing going through my mind."

At the Radisson, James had positioned himself in the corner of the room, sort of away from everyone. When all learned he was staying home, the room shifted their eyes to him and there was a brief moment of silence. Then James smiled as his friends piled on top of him, bringing him down to the plush carpet.

In Cleveland, Paxson embraced his wife as his son rejoiced. His cell phone started ringing instantly, which he grabbed as he got in the car and headed down to the arena.

At a bar in the Valley View area south of downtown that served as the official spot for the Cavs lottery party, celebrations kicked off. As cameras rolled, fans poured out emotion by bouncing, screaming and flashing homemade signs.

A few moments later, James appeared in a conference room at the Radisson in downtown Akron. He was surrounded by his high school teammates. He wore a white Nike headband with the Nike Swoosh logo. He had on a Nike black and silver sweat suit, glittering studs in each ear, and he was grinning from diamond to diamond.

"I hope I can put a lot of smiles back on the faces of the people of Cleveland," he said. "I'm not going to guarantee a championship. But we will get better every day, we will be a better team than we were last year."

He paused.

"Hopefully, the Cavs will pick me," he joked.

No doubt about that.

CHAPTER 11

"HE LOOKS LIKE AN NBA PLAYER RIGHT NOW"

Making the pick

When Miami coach Pat Riley and his staff watched tapes of LeBron James at St. Vincent-St. Mary, they could not believe they were watching a high school kid.

"He looks like an NBA player right now," they said.

They meant the 6-foot-7, 242-pound body with the 7 percent body fat. One of the hardest aspects of scouting high school kids is just that—they are kids. You don't see a body as much as a frame. How much will he grow? Is this a body that will put on weight? Will he get fat? Will he get stronger? Take any group of 18-year-olds, and look at them 10 years later. Some are fat, some skinny, some already on their way to being middle-aged and they're not even 30. But there was no guessing about what James would look like in his NBA prime—he was already that player. It was as if God decided to create the perfect basketball body. As one Heat insider said, "His game was about as developed as his body. It was so mature, so unselfish. He had great court vision. He knew how to play. Everyone in the room was convinced he'd be a huge star."

When Miami put together its draft board—ranking all the players in order starting with the best, there was no doubt who would be on top.

It was James, and the Heat had James written in ink at No. 1.

They liked Carmelo Anthony at No. 2.

Other than Detroit, it would be safe to assume nearly every team had James and Anthony as their top two players. For some reason, the Pistons fell into the trap of wanting the best big man available—even if he's not the best player. The quest for size has inspired more mistakes and downright dumb blunders than any other factor on NBA draft day. No one doubts that Pistons General Manager Joe Dumars is one of the best at his job, but even he fell into the trap when he had the No. 2 pick in 2003. He wanted a big man, and that was 7-foot Darko Milicic. He was 18 years old, from Serbia, playing in Europe. He stood out in this draft because there was no one else worthy of even being called a potential NBA center. He was young, big and breathing.

After Detroit took Milicic with the No. 2 pick, ESPN's Chad Ford wrote a scouting report that was the party line for some teams: "Darko is really one of a kind. He shoots the NBA 3 and plays with his back to the basket, so you can slot him at the 3, 4, or 5 positions. OK, a few others guys can do that, too. What sets Darko apart is his toughness in the post. You have to love a guy who has footwork to spin by an opponent but still prefers to stay lower and bang. Milicic plays in attack mode at both ends of the floor. The more you push, the more he pushes back. While he won't be asked to carry the Pistons, he's capable of doing this earlier than you think."

In Detroit, all he could carry were towels and water bottles. In three seasons, he averaged 51 points—that's 51 points for the ENTIRE SEASON. He rarely took off his warm-ups for most games. Milicic was traded to Orlando, where he played 24 minutes a game, averaging 8.0 points and 5.5 rebounds in 2006–07. He had 18 starts. The Magic wanted him to bloom. Instead, he went from a bust in Detroit to barely an average backup big man. The quickness and skills just aren't so obvious when he's facing NBA competition. Too many NBA people overlooked his lack of experience. Other than point guard, center is one of the most unforgiving positions in the NBA. The veterans just destroy rookies, who often become frustrated as they commit silly fouls and force bad shots. The Cavs' Jim Paxson saw some of that from Milicic in the European pro leagues, so he was certain it would happen in the NBA. At one point, Paxson told friends, "I just saw Darko play two games, and he got out-played both nights by Ryan Stack!"

Stack was a telephone pole of a backup center who rarely played for the Cavs from 1998–2000. After being cut, he played in Europe, where Paxson saw him against Milicic.

Here's what happens when it comes to scouting big men: So many

NBA people are looking for potential, they ignore lack of production. Milicic played two years and 38 games in the Yugoslavian pro league. In his defense, he was one of the youngest players in the league. But he averaged 7.6 points, 3.9 rebounds and was 2-of-10 on 3-pointers. How do those numbers justify much of anything in the gushing scouting reports making the rounds before the 2003 draft? Dumars figured he had a very good team and the Pistons had time to work with Milicic, perhaps turning him into a big man who could give Detroit some valuable minutes off the bench as an inside presence. He also seemed to forget that his coach at the time was Larry Brown, who is notoriously hard and intolerant of rookies, unless they happen to be instant stars. Dumars did Denver, Toronto and Miami a huge favor by picking Milicic, allowing the rest of the teams immediately drafting behind him to concentrate on the more pro-ready players. This is one decision that will always haunt Dumars. Just suppose he had selected Anthony. Put that forward on the same court with Chauncey Billups, Rip Hamilton, Ben Wallace, Tayshaun Price and just imagine how many titles could have been won. That's especially true because Detroit is a tremendous team, but prone to scoring draughts. Anthony would certain help in those situations.

Experts often say on draft day about how there is "so much talent at the top of this draft, you can't really make a mistake." Yes you can, and you can point to almost every draft and find a Darko Milicic. The players who flopped the hardest usually are big men. Consider some of the Cavs first-rounders (or products of major trades) who were nearly 7-foot: Mel Turpin, Keith Lee, DeSagana Diop, Chris Mihm and Brad Daugherty. Only Daugherty became an All-Star. Turpin and Lee were dismal failures. Diop struggled with the Cavs, then went to Dallas where he became a defensive specialist. Mihm has been a journeyman center.

While Anthony has become a major scorer with Denver, his team has not advanced farther than first round in the playoffs. Nor is he the second best player in this draft. That's Dwyane Wade, whom people in Miami will insist is equal to or even better than James.

But Miami came close to passing on Wade.

Unlike the Cavs, who knew they were picking first, Miami had to get this right—and there was plenty of room to be wrong when you're drafting No. 5.

Their draft board was James, Anthony and Milicic—in that order.

Yes, Milicic was No. 3, as this was before the Heat had traded for Shaquille O'Neal. They wanted a big man. If he had slipped to No. 5, it's possible Miami would have called the name of Darko Milicic on draft day 2003, and there would have been no title in 2006.

As the Heat coaches knew back then, "We were a non-factor in the NBA, just like the Cavs. We had not been down that long, but we were way down."

On draft day, Miami watched James go to the Cavs, Milicic to Detroit, Anthony to Denver.

Toronto was picking fourth.

Miami had a major debate rating the next group of players. The scouts and player personnel types strongly favored Wade, a 6-foot-3 guard from Marquette. Riley wanted size, if at all possible. He was very interested in another big man, 7-footer Chris Kaman from Central Michigan. Remember how it works with so many teams on draft day. When you don't have a big man, you find yourself nearly blinded by the height. "You can't win without a good big man," is conventional basketball wisdom. But you'll never win if you skip a good guard or small forward because you want the best big man available, even if he's not all that good. Kaman has been much better than Milicic, but he's barely an average starting center. In 2005–06, he averaged 11.9 points, 9.6 rebounds and earned a $50 million contract. He followed that up with 10.1 points, 7.8 rebounds for the Los Angeles Clippers, who picked him sixth—right behind Wade. The next two selections—point guards Kirk Hinrich (Chicago) and T.J. Ford (Milwaukee)—have made bigger impacts on teams than Kaman. That's especially true of Ford, who was traded to Toronto where he teamed up with fellow 2003 draft class member Bosh to lead the Raptors to a playoff berth in 2007, helping Sam Mitchell earn Coach of the Year honors.

In the end, Miami rated Georgia Tech forward Chris Bosh at No. 4, and they had Wade at No. 5. Their first four players were selected in the top four, so they grabbed Wade—not knowing they had just picked a superstar who would be the key to them winning a title in 2006. Miami had to convert Wade from a shooting guard at Marquette to a point guard—or at least, a guard with enough ballhandling skills to start an offense. Riley decided not to coach in 2003–04, the rookie years for Wade and James. He turned the team over to trusted assistant Stan

Van Gundy, who started Wade from opening day of rookie camp at point guard. Riley remained in the team's front office. At the time, no one knew Wade would rival James for the best of the Class of 2003. Nor did anyone realize their rivalry began in James' first pro games, when he was with the Cavs summer league rookie/free agent team in Orlando. All the attention was on James. Usually, summer league games are played in front of family, friends, agents, team officials and European pro scouts getting a line on what players may be cut by the NBA—so they can convince them to play overseas. But the hype over James made this an event, although little attention was paid to Wade. In fact, Riley just gushed about the Cavs' top pick.

"LeBron is a Pied Piper, like Magic," he said. "People just want to be around him. Other players follow his lead. He is just an incredible talent, and look at what he's done for the [Cavaliers'] season tickets. There are a few players that come along each generation. There was Bird and Magic. Then came Michael [Jordan], and now maybe it's this kid's turn."

A prophetic part of that game came in the final minutes. Coaching the Heat summer league team was Stan Van Gundy, and he wanted to see what Wade would do in the final minute of a close game. He put the ball in his rookie's hands, and told Wade to attack James. He did, scoring what became the winning basket. He would win several shootouts with James over the next few years.

It's revealing to look not just at the 2003 draft which changed the futures of several franchise . . . the Cavs with LeBron . . . Miami with Wade . . . Detroit still a power, but passing on Wade, Bosh and Anthony . . . Denver improving with Anthony . . . Bosh making Toronto a playoff team.

But also consider the roster that James joined with the Cavs in 2003. As pointed out, the Cavs didn't stagger to that lottery-bound 17-65 record by accident. They were designed to be bad. Make that terrible. Make the Cavs a team that put James in a deeper hole than any superstar entering the league since 1970. That's why the comparisons with Jordan, Bird and Magic Johnson have to be put in some historical context when comparing James to them.

1. Why is this man smiling? Ted Stepien traded away five consecutive first-round draft picks and nearly killed pro basketball in Cleveland. *(Cleveland Cavaliers)*

2. Gordon Gund bought the Cavaliers from Ted Stepien in 1983 and saved basketball for Cleveland. *(Akron Beacon Journal/Karen Schiely)*

3. General Manager Jim Paxson had to tear down the team so the franchise would be in a position to get LeBron James. *(Cleveland Cavaliers)*

4. The Cavaliers wanted a star. They got Shawn Kemp. *(Akron Beacon Journal/Phil Masturzo)*

5. LeBron goes national. *Sports Illustrated* discovered James as a high school junior and dubbed him "The Chosen One" on his first major magazine cover, in 2002. *(Akron Beacon Journal/Phil Masturzo)*

6. LeBron with his mother, Gloria James, and mentor Eddie Jackson in 2002. Eyebrows were raised by Jackson's efforts to promote LeBron to the shoe companies while LeBron was still playing high school basketball. *(Akron Beacon Journal/Phil Masturzo)*

7. Cavs representative Warren Thaler was the first to know Cleveland had gotten LeBron. This image was captured on a closed-circuit TV monitor just as the final ball dropped in the lottery. *(Cleveland Cavaliers)*

8. Before he even played for the team, LeBron got a standing ovation from Cleveland fans at a draft-night party at Gund Arena. *(Akron Beacon Journal/Ed Suba Jr.)*

9. LeBron signals to St. Vincent-St. Mary teammates and coaches, and friends, moments after being selected as the Cleveland Cavaliers' first pick in the 2003 NBA Draft. *(Akron Beacon Journal/Phil Masturzo)*

10. Nike CEO Phil Knight (right), Nike executive Lynn Merritt (center), and sports deal-maker William "Wes" Wesley (left) are among many businesspeople watching LeBron's success closely. Here they attend LeBron's first home game for the Cavs. *(Akron Beacon Journal)*

11. LeBron is congratulated by Cavaliers GM Jim Paxson as team owner Gordon Gund smiles in the background at the press conference announcing James as the Rookie of the Year in 2004. *(Akron Beacon Journal/Mike Cardew)*

12. New owner Dan Gilbert brought Danny Ferry back to Cleveland in 2005 to stabilize his franchise. Ferry wasn't sure he wanted the job at first, but he couldn't pass up the chance to build a team around LeBron. *(Akron Beacon Journal/Phil Masturzo)*

13. Making it light up like Vegas—a Cavs game at Quicken Loans Arena reflects the show-manship brought to the team by Dan Gilbert. *(Cleveland Cavaliers)*

14. In a pregame ritual patterned after Michael Jordan's, LeBron throws resin in the air. *(Ron Kuntz)*

15. In order to keep LeBron, the Cavs knew they had to keep Zydrunas Ilgauskas (left) and add talent such as Larry Hughes (right). *(Ron Kuntz)*

16. Dan Gilbert sunk $25 million into a practice palace for LeBron and the Cavaliers in Independence, Ohio, part of an aggressive campaign to keep LeBron and attract free agents. *(Akron Beacon Journal/Phil Masturzo)*

17. Matching the coach with the player—the Cavs' front office hired Mike Brown in 2005 to lead LeBron and the team to a championship. He became their sixth coach in six years. *(Akron Beacon Journal/Phil Masturzo)*

18. A nine-story billboard across from Quicken Loans Arena suggests the size of the impact LeBron and the revived Cavaliers have had on the downtown area. *(Cleveland Cavaliers)*

19. Once upon a time, good seats were *always* available. In 2007, ticketless fans stood outside "The Q" to watch Game 6 of the 2007 Eastern Conference playoff series on large video monitors. *(Akron Beacon Journal/Ken Love)*

20. Something not seen often in Cleveland: a championship trophy. LeBron celebrates winning the 2007 Eastern Conference Finals. *(Ron Kuntz)*

22. At last, another banner for the rafters. There's room for more. *(Ron Kuntz)*

21. Zydrunas Ilgauskas was there through the hard times. Here they hug after beating Detroit in the 2007 Eastern Conference Finals. *(Ron Kuntz)*

CHAPTER 12

"ALL HE EVER TALKED ABOUT WAS WANTING TO WIN"

LeBron starts over

The moment Russ Granik announced that Memphis (which then became Detroit thanks to a trade) had the second pick, the phones began ringing at the Gund Arena ticket offices.

"Operators are standing by to take ticket orders," Cavs radio broadcaster Joe Tait often said during games. He would sometimes add, "Why don't they let those people sit down? Why do they have to stand by?"

On this night, they were coming out of their chairs.

The Cavs had a dozen sales people ready to handle calls from fans. They were as overwhelmed as a 5-foot-9 high school kid trying to stop James from dunking. Phones didn't ring, they seemed to scream.

"We had people buying season tickets at 2 a.m.," said Tad Carper, the team's vice president of communications. "Our sales staff stayed there all night and into the next morning, answering phones. This was back before you could buy tickets on-line. The highest priced tickets sold first. That usually happens when a team is winning, or there's a sudden surge of interest. People want the best tickets available, and they are willing to pay for them."

Remember the complaints about the high price of Cavs tickets when the team was losing? They stopped with the drafting of James. Or at least, they didn't matter because the market for tickets was so hot, and the demand for the prime seats so high. Even before the Cavs went to the 2007 NBA Finals, the Cavs were selling about 150 floor seats for an average of $700 each per game. They had a few seats right next to the bench going for $1,700 per night. Carper said they could easily sell more than 300 of these floor seats per game, if they could find room for the chairs. That's why they have moved every media member possible away from the floor to seats higher in the arena. And it all began with James on lottery night. At the end of the 17-win, 2002–03 season, the Cavs had about 2,000 season tickets. They never will reveal the exactly number, but talking to people who worked in the ticket department during that sad season said 2,000 was a decent estimate. Certainly no more. They announced an average attendance for the season of 11,497—dead last in the NBA. By the time James played his first regular season game with the Cavs, season's tickets were up to about 10,000. Group sales were up. Suite sales were up. Television and radio ratings were about to soar. The Cavs have about 1,500 tickets near the ceiling in the $10 range for most games. They were the *last* to be sold—fans literally wanting to be as close to James as possible at the games, and willing to pay big money to do so. Across the arena, most tickets were raised between $2 to $5 per game, the average price being close to $50.

"Not long after the draft, we had LeBron, his mother and some of his friends to the arena for dinner," said Gordon Gund. "I was impressed with how close he was to his mother, and how he dealt with his friends. He didn't lord over them, they just seemed to be his buddies. And they didn't put him on a pedestal, either. He was still very young, but I could sense his maturity."

Paxson said that while he'd seen James play in person several times, the 6-foot-5 former NBA player and general manager had never stood next to James until that night. The perceptive 18-year-old looked at Paxson and said, "You didn't think I was this big, did you?"

Paxson laughed, because that's exactly what he was thinking.

"I couldn't believe any 18-year-old could have a mature body like that," said Paxson. "He was very personable that night. I really liked his mother, and from the beginning, Gloria was a real asset in helping us with LeBron. As for LeBron, he had a real sense of himself, and didn't seem overwhelmed by anything that was happening."

It was as if James were born into a royal family and always knew that one day, the castle and the throne would be his. He wasn't arrogant about it. He just expected it to happen. When it did, there was no reason for surprise. It was part of the plan. He never said this. This is rare for a young man who didn't come from a basketball family—it's not like his father or brothers were great players and coaches and he grew up next to them in the gym. But somewhere early in his high school career, James just *knew* that one day—there would be a day like this. A day when the NBA draft would come and his name would be called first. A day when he'd be at Gund Arena, not as a young fan with NBA dreams bouncing across his brain, but as an honored guest of the team owner.

Gund and Paxson could feel it that night of the first dinner and meeting—James was the real thing. Suddenly, Gund and Paxson felt a new form of pressure. The fans were coming, the national spotlight was on James and the franchise. The team had just won 17 games, and fired interim coach Keith Smart. It took a lot for the Cavaliers to become that terrible, and even adding a talent like James was not about to fix everything.

The burden wasn't just on James, it was on them.

"We just had to get the right people around LeBron," said Gund. "We needed to get the right coach, the right players. Somehow, we had to manage the expectations, which were so high—almost out of control. I admit, I was worried about it. I didn't want LeBron under too much pressure."

Paxson's greatest weakness as a general manager was selecting and dealing with his coaches. In four years, he had been through Randy Wittman, John Lucas and Keith Smart. This wasn't like the 2002-03 season when the goal was hit bottom to have some hope of getting lucky in the lottery. They were lucky, now it was time to be good.

The Cavs went into the LeBron Lottery without a coach. Not long after, they had two experienced candidates in Paul Silas and Jeff Van Gundy. Both had a track record of reasonable success. While neither had won a title, both had coached teams that had advanced past the first round of the playoffs. Van Gundy reached the 1999 Finals with the New York Knicks. In 2002-03, Van Gundy had taken the season off, as he was mentally exhausted after coaching in New York. Now refreshed, he was ready for a new challenge. The Cavs were interested, and so were the Houston Rockets. Silas had led the New Orleans Hornets to a 44-38 record and to the second round of the 2002 playoffs. He was shocked when fired, as were most executives in the NBA. The general consensus was Silas had squeezed the most any coach could out of spunky but not very talented teams. He was not the reason the Hornets failed to advance any deeper in the post-season. But in the modern NBA where the average coach lasts about three years with a team, Silas was canned. He was extremely interested in the Cavs job, especially with James on the roster.

"We needed a veteran coach to stabilize things," said Gund. "We were torn between Van Gundy and Silas. We knew that LeBron had to learn things the right way as a rookie, or it would be much harder for him down the line."

Like Gund, Paxson saw tremendous merit in both Van Gundy and Silas.

"My only concern with Van Gundy was that he had resigned or whatever [after 19 games with the Knicks in 2001–02 when they were 10-9 and ended up 30-52]," said Paxson. "But overall, he was a respected coach and did a good job in New York. My concern with Silas was if we got really good, could he lead us to a championship? I didn't say no. But I also didn't know if he could. Van Gundy had been to the Finals. He didn't win, but he got a team there. Maybe he could grow with LeBron. Van Gundy was interested, but not all the way. He had other opportunities. I liked the fact that Silas had been a former player, that he was respected by a lot of people in the league. I sensed he could bring stability. Gordon met with Paul twice, and we decided to go with him."

Silas, a huge presence, a bear of a man at 6-foot-6 and 260 pounds, played in the NBA for 16 years and was on three championship teams. He twice was an All-Star. He was an unselfish, relentless power forward with little interest in scoring—unless it was needed—and had a tremendous commitment to doing what was needed to help his team win. He set picks to free up teammates for shots. Did he ever set picks. He was wide enough to set a pick on a noon day summer sun and make it seem like midnight. He was strong enough to set a pick on a charging bull and turn it into hamburger. He was smart enough to knock opponents over with a slight shove in the back, a nudge of the elbow, a toss of the hip. He rebounded. Did he ever rebound. To Silas, rebounding was like breathing. Rebounding was effort. Rebounding was heart. Rebounding was what his teams would do. His Hornets had led the league in rebounding, despite not having any premier big men. The idea would be that James and his young teammates would now have a coach with instant credibility, and the NBA lifer would not be overwhelmed by taking over a 17-win team with an 18-year-old star and a boiling pot of expectations that would be impossible to be met.

"I believed Paul was strong enough to keep the players focused on the team and also keep LeBron centered on the team," said Gund. "He did that."

The starting lineup early in the season was Darius Miles, Ricky Davis, Carlos Boozer, James and Zydrunas Ilgauskas.

The Cavs had many flaws on the roster, one of the biggest being no point guard. Paxson had signed journeyman Kevin Ollie as a free agent, but it was clear he lacked the talent to start. Silas tried to have Miles play point guard—and that was a disaster. Silas didn't want to put the ball in James' hands as an 18-year-old who wasn't programmed for the point, despite his obvious passing skills.

When the Cavs opened the season in Sacramento, James served notice that he would not be an ordinary rookie. The box score was a stunner: 25 points, 9 assists, 6 rebounds, 4 steals. He did most of that as a point guard, not his natural position. The Cavs lost 106-93 to the Kings, but a national cable TV audience had seen the birth of a star. They also saw James pass up an open lay-up, waiting for teammate Ricky Davis to trail—and then, he delivered a perfect pass that Davis transformed into an ESPN highlight dunk. The first thought was, "Ricky Davis would never give up two easy points on a play like that." The next thought was, "Davis probably doesn't appreciate what James just did, how he's trying hard to fit in." After the game, James simply said, "That's what a point guard does." He had decided the point guard-challenged Cavs needed him to help out at the position.

Veteran James' watchers also used this game as evidence to what they had been saying for a few years, "LeBron averaged 31 points in high school, and he scored 25 in his first NBA game. Isn't it obvious he could have averaged 50 in high school? That his priority really is on winning?" Many of the approximately 300 media members at that game had to agree. So did celebrities such as Reggie Jackson, Dusty Baker and Terrell Owens, who attended the game to see James' debut.

But it was obvious that the Cavs had a real hangover from that 17-65 team. There was little defense, even less consideration of team play. It galled Silas, and the coach knew he had to do something.

"I didn't know how good LeBron would be, I just knew he had potential," said Silas. "My goal was to come in as a teacher. I just wanted to know if I would get the time to teach the players as we worked to get the right guys around LeBron. Early on, I had to get their respect."

Silas mentioned an early season clash with Ira Newble, who came into the coaches office after a game in Atlanta. The Cavs had lost. Newble had taken five shots and missed them all. He complained about his lack of playing time.

"I knew there would be growing pains, and this was one of them," said Silas. "I was talking to Ira, and he walked out on me before I was finished."

Silas roared out of the coach's office into the hallway, where media members were talking to players after the game. Silas was like an enraged bear, scowling, growling and spewing out some words not meant for a family audience. He put a couple of X-rated adjectives around the word "hip-hop" to describe Newble's attitude. A shocked Newble stood there, not saying a word. The media wrote down the exchange, and reported it.

"I wished it didn't happen in front of the media, but it did," said Silas. "I felt there was no respect. If I let it go, I was dead. Ira apologized to me the next day, and we've been good ever since."

Not long after that, Silas suspended Ricky Davis and bench warmer Michael Stewart because he didn't like their attitudes. He and Paxson talked about trades that had to be made.

"From that first game, I knew LeBron was special," said Silas. "The whole world was watching how he'd respond and he came through with flying colors. At that time, I was playing him some at point guard because we had no one else. He didn't complain about that. He didn't complain about anything, even though he was playing the wrong position because we had no one else. Being as young as he was and not having played point before, this wasn't helping his game much. I was asking him to do something that would be hard for a five-year veteran to do—changing positions. But all LeBron ever talked about was wanting to win."

So Silas went to Paxson and said changes had to be made. The general manager knew it. The Cavs opened the season with three games on the road, all losses. James' pro debut at Gund Arena was against Denver and Carmelo Anthony. The two young players were being hyped as the Larry Bird and Magic Johnson of this year, one in the East and one in the West, who would lead their teams to meet each other in the Finals. Obviously, that was a ridiculous notion. Bird and Johnson were players for the ages. Still, the likes of Ken Griffey Jr. and rapper Jay-Z showed up in Cleveland for the game. So did Phil Knight, the CEO of Nike who had dished out more than $115 million to sign James and Anthony as corporate spokesmen. And so did a sellout crowd, who greeted the team with the NBA's worst record with a standing ovation.

The last time James and Anthony had met—in a high school game—the two scored a combined 70 points. Anthony's team won the game; James won the personal scoring duel, 36-34. On this night in front of his home crowd as a new pro, James was nervous. He scored only seven points, was 3-of-11 shooting and his field goals were two dunks and a lay-up. He still snared 11 rebounds.

What really bothered Silas was that James had a good night passing, with seven assists—but that was more than the other four starters combined. Silas never said it, but he believed Davis was poisoning the team. He had no interest in sharing the spotlight or the ball with James. His defense was a rumor. He was simply playing for his own statistics.

The Cavs were 6-19 when they traded Davis along with Chris Mihm, Michael Stewart and a second-rounder to Boston for veterans Eric Williams, Tony Battie and a young player named Kedrick Brown. A month later on January 21, 2004, the Cavs finally found a point guard, sending a confused Darius Miles (who hated playing in Cleveland) to Portland for veteran Jeff McInnis. While McInnis was a tempera-mental point guard who eventually did self-destruct, he was on his best behavior that season. The Cavs finished 29-28 after Davis was dumped. James flourished, winning the Rookie of the Year award, av-eraging 21 points, 5.9 assists and 5.5 rebounds. The only other players to average at least 20 points, five assists and five rebounds as rookies were Michael Jordan and Oscar Robertson. James had 13 games of at least 30 points. No player coming directly from high school ever came close to putting together this type of season.

When the season was over, Silas marveled, "He'll be a great player. He averaged 21 points, which is off the charts. He needs to work on his outside shot. We want him to improve his defense . . . but he came on like gangbusters, didn't he? He never hit a wall [of fatigue]. He stayed humble. He didn't antagonize other players. No question about it, he can be one of the best ever. He's so coachable, and he was under so much pressure. We'd show up at a hotel at two in the morning [flying in from another city] and there would be 30 people waiting for him."

Silas pulled James from a late-season game, telling his star as he sat on the bench, "You're not getting back on defense, so I'm sitting your butt down."

James wasn't pleased, but he refused to show up his coach. He sat and waited for a chance to get back into the game. That's something else that excited the Cavs during James' rookie season—he wanted to please his coach. He refused to play the star card, and made a major effort to get along with his teammates. It was much the same approach he took at St. Vincent-St. Mary's.

After his rookie year, James often talked about the team's success. He was happy that the Cavs went from 17 to 35 victories: "That was my goal, for us to get better."

Paxson mentioned how trading Miles was right for the team, but Miles also was James' best friend.

"I went to LeBron and told him how we were trading Darius for McInnis," said Paxson.

At the time, James was playing a computer game. He glanced up for a moment, then said, "We do need a point guard."

Then he went back to his game.

"LeBron never told me to trade for this guy, or get rid of someone," said Paxson. "He really was supportive."

It's tempting to disregard much of what James says as basic clichés, to think he's simply trying to avoid giving quotes that might hurt him with his fans, his team or teammates. But James really does put a priority on winning. That became obvious over his first four Cavs seasons as he and the team improved each year. He really does want to do and say the right things. James proved it to the Cavs front office when he declined to take part in the NBA dunk contest during All-Star weekend. The league wanted it because his presence would improve TV ratings. Nike wanted it because if James won the contest—and he probably would have—it would have increased shoe sales and made James an even a bigger name.

James told the NBA the same thing he told Paxson, "I look at myself as a basketball player, not a dunker. I don't want my stage to be the dunk contest."

But he was not a normal NBA rookie, regardless of how he tried to make that happen.

"After the draft, I called [Minnesota general manager] Kevin McHale to ask him what we should do since he'd had Kevin Garnett coming straight from high school to the pros—and Garnett had adjusted so well," said Paxson. "McHale said one of the differences between Garnett and LeBron is Garnett went to high school in Chicago. LeBron is from the Cleveland area. McHale said early on they let some of Garnett's friends travel with the team. Part of the problem with that is once you start, it's hard to draw the line. If you do it for one player, then you have to do it for everyone. And suddenly, you have all these extra people traveling with the team. McHale said after a few years Garnett didn't have people around as much."

James' companions were Randy Mims, Maverick Carter and a few others. Eventually, the Cavs allowed Mims to travel with the team, then gave him the title of "Player Liaison." Mostly, he was James' personal assistant. His hotel room was near James. He was there to make sure James was not overwhelmed by the public, and there to help James— already a national celebrity at 18—deal with the various appearances he needed to make for his sponsors. Paxson said he talked to several of the Cavaliers veteran players before allowing Mims to travel with the team. "They agreed that there were only a few guys in the league who really needed someone on the road with them, but LeBron was one because of all the pressures on him," said Paxson. "LeBron had first asked Gordon [Gund] about Randy Mims traveling, and then Gordon and I talked about it. LeBron never demanded it, he just mentioned it would help him."

Gund said, "When you have a special young player, you want him to know his views are respected. You want to make sure that things haven't suddenly gotten off track. You want him to feel genuinely a part of the organization, not just on the court."

The best players have always received perks, going back to the days when Babe Ruth was allowed to play himself into shape during spring training and certain stars had private rooms on the road when other players shared rooms. Most players didn't mind—if the stars produced and didn't flaunt their exalted status. James was able to do that.

"Guys challenged LeBron in practice," said Silas. "It was tough for him. But he went right back at them. That's another thing I loved about LeBron—he didn't back down from anyone. He had to grow into it, but you could see it happening in games. I had to get on him to shoot sometimes when he was open, not to be shy. That was another part of his growth. He knew he was the focal point of the team, and the guys kept relying on him more to get things done. When he said things in huddles, by the end of the season, guys were listening to him. He went from a rookie who had to show everyone that he was a player . . . Well, he showed them. He put up the numbers. And he started to take on the leadership."

All of that before he turned 20, which made it all the more impressive to Silas and Paxson.

"The only thing I thought LeBron needed to do after his rookie year was learn how the best player on the team must compete and lead every day in practice," said Paxson. "LeBron played hard. But he wouldn't always stay after practice for extra work. He'd do his thing with the media and go home. Other players saw that. When your best player works extra, then the others tend to follow."

Paxson talked to James about that, about how the teammates of Michael Jordan marveled at how intense Jordan was in practice, and how he "made practices harder than games." All that work and effort in practice made the Bulls of the Jordan Era very tough late in close games.

"I could see LeBron improving in that area by his second year, and he's getting even better now," said Paxson. "He picks things up."

That first season with James, the Cavs' attendance rose from 11,497 per game to 18,288. They went from the worst team in the league to one not far from contention. Not only was James a legitimate star, but the Cavs seemed to have developed an excellent sidekick for their prodigy in Carlos Boozer, who averaged 15 points and 11 rebounds playing next to James. It was only his second season, and one of the goals for the summer of 2004 was to make sure James and Boozer stayed together for a long time. No one would ever guess that when the two young stars walked off the court on April 14, 2004, they would never play together with the Cavaliers again.

CHAPTER 13

"YOU CAN TRUST ME ON THAT"

A bad deal with Carlos Boozer

This is the story of how the Cavaliers thought they had their guy to play with LeBron James—and how they lost him.

It began on a sunny afternoon on June 30, 2004, when Carlos Boozer and his party walked away from a meeting at Gund Arena. The Cavaliers were sure the power forward would be a part of the team for six more years. On the sixth floor of the arena's executive offices, Gordon Gund and Jim Paxson were convinced they were on the verge of making a deal that would satisfy everyone, a rarity in today's NBA. What Boozer really thought will always be open to debate.

The point was the Cavs believed that they and Boozer wanted the same thing—a way to keep him with the team. In Carlos Boozer, Paxson thought he had found the perfect on-court companion to LeBron James. James could be Mr. Outside, or Mr. Whatever He Wanted. One thing was certain, Boozer would not get in the way. The power forward pounded the boards. He could make an open medium range jumper. He had a nice hook shot near the basket. Coming from Duke, he was well coached, very disciplined and seemingly interested in winning first. He was bright, polite and one of Gordon Gund's favorite players.

Boozer was a second-round pick by Paxson in 2002, a year before anyone knew he'd be a key player with LeBron James. Little was said when Boozer came to the Cavs, other than he followed two previous Duke product who failed to live up to expectations in Cleveland—guard Trajan Langdon and forward Danny Ferry. Boozer was listed at 6-foot-9, 260 pounds. He probably was closer to 6-foot-8, and some scouts thought he was too short to be a power forward, too slow to be a small forward. They underrated him because they believed, like many Duke players, he'd peaked in college and benefited from Coach Mike Krzyzewski putting him in a system that accented his strengths, hid his weaknesses.

The Cavs didn't know it at the time, but Boozer was very angry and resentful about slipping into the second round and having 34 names called before his. Being a second-rounder cost Boozer both prestige and money. The lower you are drafted, the less you are paid as the NBA has a "slotting" system, assigning a certain salary to each draft position. A determined Boozer rose from second-round draft pick status and the end of coach John Lucas' bench to average 10 points and 7.5 rebounds, and was named to the NBA's All-Rookie Team. The success just made Boozer even more upset about his contract. He had signed a two-year guaranteed deal with an option for a third year. This was a rare deal for a second-round pick. Such players seldom receive more than one-year contracts under the slotting system, but the Cavs went two years. Boozer was paid nearly $1 million split over the first two seasons.

The Cavs had an option for a third year, in which Boozer's salary would be $695,000 for the 2004–05 season. Boozer made a major step forward in his second season, averaging 15 points and 11 rebounds. The Cavs knew he would be wildly underpaid with the $695,000 option. But if they failed to exercise the option, then Boozer would become a free agent.

A former second-round pick named Gilbert Arenas had just received a six-year, $65 million deal after his second season, making Boozer even more anxious about his contract. Of course, Arenas became a free agent—and could sign with anyone, giving him tremendous leverage to work a deal. Boozer had none of that, because of the option he'd agreed to in his original contract. Boozer was represented by the sports management group SFX, founded by Arn Tellem. His agent was Rob Pelinka, who approached the Cavs about what it would take to let Boozer out of the final year of the contract. In the spring of 2004, Boozer talked to the *Akron Beacon Journal's* Brian Windhorst for a story that ran under the headline, "Honorable Boozer a Bargain For Cavs; Power Forward Willing to Wait For His Big Payday." It's important to look back on this story, because it was one of the reasons the Cavs acted as they did with Boozer that summer:

A game-day practice was ending earlier this month in Detroit, and Jeff McInnis was looking for a little action from Carlos Boozer.

McInnis' North Carolina Tar Heels were playing Boozer's Duke Blue Devils that night, and a wager was at hand.

"Not too much," Boozer cautioned, "I don't have that much money."

For many fans, that might sound like ridiculous elitism. Boozer doesn't have trouble making the mortgage payment every month. But this is NBA basketball we're talking about and, in those terms, Boozer is a pauper. McInnis makes roughly six times what Boozer pulls down. Teammate Zydrunas Ilgauskas makes more in four games of work ($600,000) than Boozer will all season ($563,000). It won't take Johnnie Cochran to win an argument that Boozer is already one of the game's best power forwards and that he's woefully under compensated for it. The heartwarming side of Boozer's story is that he's risen to this status from being a lowly second-round draft pick. The reality is that he's still paid like an also-ran.

General manager Jim Paxson landed a whopper deal with Boozer, signing him to a two-year contract with a team option for next season that will pay him the NBA minimum. Next year, he's slated to make slightly less than $700,000. But Boozer, his agent, and the Cavaliers are all thinking ahead to a potential deal this summer that could keep him in Cleveland far into the future. The complexities of this issue are massive and so are the stakes. Keeping Boozer for the long haul is nearly as vital as making sure LeBron James is around, too.

"There are people doing what I'm doing that are making eight or 10 million a year," Boozer said. "I want to be able to take care of my family. I want a big house. These are things I dream about. These are things that have always motivated me."

The rules surrounding the collective bargaining agreement say that if the Cavaliers want to give Boozer a rich contract this summer to reward him and keep him for years to come, they will have to decline their team option on him. By doing so, that would put Boozer out on the open market as an unrestricted free agent and there are a dozen teams that could pay him more than the Cavaliers.

That would be a bad short-term business move, considering the club could have Boozer as a great bargain for next season, too, and then he'd be a restricted free agent. Then they could match any offer for 2005–06, the salary cap be darned because of what's called "Bird rights." Making him fulfill his contract is the best course by the book.

What Boozer and his agent are proposing is to make a handshake deal where he would agree to a new contract that the Cavaliers can afford under next year's cap and then sign it moments after becoming a free agent, forgetting the open market. This is a way for Boozer to get his millions now instead of two years from now. In return, the Cavaliers would likely pay him less than they would by giving him his millions in two years. It is also a risk that Boozer wouldn't bolt for more money somewhere else this summer.

Not only that but such unspoken deals are technically illegal under NBA rules and the Cavaliers could be punished for such an infraction.

"Absolutely, that is something I am willing to do. I am an honorable person," Boozer said. "We have a great foundation here. My wife likes it here. I like it here. I am fine with sharing the spotlight with LeBron. Everything is going in the right direction for me. I think there is a big possibility to get something done this summer. This stuff that we're talking about will probably be worked out before next season."

Boozer wants fans to know that he's not complaining about his pay, he's not demanding a raise or threatening to hold out. If the parties can't come to terms this summer, which is likely for a deal this complex, Boozer will honor his commitment and wait for his money.

"I'm making a lot of money compared to the average person, but in the NBA it is chump change, especially the way I'm playing," he said. "I feel like I am going to get what I deserve. That contract I signed got me motivated. Right now I'm going on the right path and I want to keep it that way."

With that in mind, the Cavs thought they could make a deal that would allow both sides to walk away happy. On June 30, 2004, the principals gathered around a Fortune 500-style boardroom table at Gund Arena. Pelinka had flown in from Los Angeles. He sat on one side with Boozer and his wife, CeCe, a Duke graduate who had experience working for sports management giant IMG. Gordon Gund flew in by his private jet from his offices in Princeton, N.J. He joined Paxson and members of his staff on the other side of the table. The meeting opened with Gund telling Boozer how valuable he was to the Cavaliers' franchise and their fan base. Gund was perhaps closer to Boozer than any other Cavaliers player. To Gund, players like Boozer and center Zydrunas Ilgauskas represented the transition the organization was trying to make. Each time Gund visited the Cavaliers during the season—either in Cleveland or at road games in Boston, New Jersey, New York or Philadelphia—he spent time talking with Boozer. Paxson informed Pelinka and the Boozers that the Cavaliers were considering letting Boozer out of the option year. That decision had to be finalized by midnight that evening.

Paxson explained to them that after losing Jason Kapono in the recent expansion draft and making a trade to acquire Sasha Pavlovic, the team's payroll would be $43,434,000 next season. That would put the Cavaliers within $3 million of the salary cap, expected to be announced the next week. Paxson said that if the Cavaliers allowed Boozer to become a free agent, the only thing the team could do was offer him something referred to as the maximum "Early Bird" contract. That would be a deal starting at $5 million that would increase 12.5 percent each year for six years, making it worth around $40 million. This was not a contract offer to Boozer, just an explanation of what the Cavaliers' salary cap constraint would be. Paxson told Boozer that the team would not make any trades or other player moves to try and get drastically under the salary cap to attempt to offer more.

As a part of the goodwill gesture of not picking up the option, Boozer and Pelinka would have to calm the fan base by making public statements on July 1 of his intention to return to the Cavaliers. They would not be saying they officially had agreed to a deal. That would be in violation of NBA rules because it came before July 1. Pelinka had brought a copy of the NBA's collective bargaining agreement and referred to the contract rules and read from it several times. The Cavaliers made it clear to Boozer that as many as seven other NBA teams could offer him more money and the team was taking a risk. Gund told Boozer that he didn't want him to commit to a contract that he would regret signing a few years down the road. The Cavaliers reminded Boozer that by picking up the $695,000 option, the team would be able to sign him to a contract larger than the $40 million deal after the 2004–05 season because they would not be under NBA salary cap restraints. But Carlos and CeCe, who only a few days earlier were looking at expensive houses in the affluent east-side Cleveland suburb of Bratenahl, said they wanted security now. They understood there was a limit, due to the league's salary cap rules, on what the Cavaliers could offer, but they wanted to remain in Cleveland. At least that's how several members of the Cavs present at the meeting recalled the conversation. Then Boozer and Gund spoke to each other. As they talked, they appeared to come to an understanding they both thought would eventually lead to a deal.

The parties broke and had separate discussions. It was a tense 10-minute period that might be remembered as one of the most crucial moments in Cavaliers history that didn't take place on a basketball court. Gund asked Paxson if he thought the Cavaliers could trust Boozer. Paxson pointed out that Pelinka was present when the Boozers said they knew it was possible to get a larger offer than the Cavaliers could put on the table after July 1—but they still preferred to stay in Cleveland. At that time, Paxson and Gund agreed to allow Boozer to become a restricted free agent, if that was what he wanted.

The Boozers and Pelinka came back into the room and said they indeed wanted to be let out of the contract. They knew they could not make a deal on that day, but Pelinka said he was sure he could work out a deal with Paxson after July 1. Paxson promptly left the room and went to his office, where he had prepared a "qualifying offer," which is part of the procedure in making a player a restricted free agent. Under NBA rules, all qualifying offers have to be issued before July 1. The meeting then broke up, midnight passed, and Carlos Boozer was no longer a Cavalier.

On July 1, the Cavaliers stunned the NBA by revealing they'd not picked up Boozer's option. Boozer and Pelinka granted interviews to the Associated Press stating their preference to re-sign with the Cavaliers. But, in retrospect, they did not issue any guarantees.

"I want to be in Cleveland, I want to be with the Cavaliers," Boozer told the Associated Press. "Now it's up to my agent and the Cavs to work things out."

"Carlos and his wife, CeCe, made it clear to me that they are very comfortable with the Cavaliers organization," Pelinka told the AP. "I'm confident [Paxson] and I will continue to have conversations and we'll be able to work something out."

That afternoon, Utah Jazz owner Larry H. Miller made a previously scheduled phone call to a reporter in Salt Lake City. During the course of the conversation, the reporter asked Miller if the Jazz had any interest in Boozer. Until that moment, Miller was unaware the Cavaliers hadn't picked up Boozer's option. Miller told the reporter he was planning to call Jazz Vice President Kevin O'Connor to have him look into Boozer's availability.

On July 2, Boozer disconnected a cell phone that the Cavaliers and media had been using to contact him. On July 3, the Boozers were telling people that there was no deal with the Cavaliers in place. Over the July 4th weekend, the Golden State Warriors came to an agreement with center Adonal Foyle on a five-year, $41.6 million contract, a deal worth more per year than what Boozer could sign for with the Cavaliers under NBA rules. It was shocking, as the 6-foot-10 Foyle had averaged fewer than four points and four rebounds per game. Then Utah signed an offer sheet with Detroit Pistons forward Mehmet Okur for six years and nearly $50 million. He averaged 5.9 points and 9.6 rebounds. Boozer kept thinking, "I'm better than these guys and they're going to get more money than me." Once again, he feared he was about to be cheated by signing a deal with the Cavaliers. With contract values soaring, especially for big men, Boozer getting a six-year, $40 million deal would certainly be lower than his market value. If the player signed for such a figure, it would affect the agent, too. Potential clients might be told that Boozer had signed what was perceived as a "bad contract."

This was what the Cavaliers feared, that Boozer would be tempted to look elsewhere.

On Monday, July 5, Pelinka called Paxson and told him the Boozers had decided to test the market. He took calls from several teams and found interest in the Denver Nuggets and the Utah Jazz. On Wednesday, July 7, the Jazz prepared their huge offer sheet.

To ensure they wouldn't lose Boozer, the Jazz wanted to "frontload" the offer, meaning they would pay a large salary in the first year to make it harder for the Cavaliers to try to match.

Another factor, but not a big one, was a meeting between Boozer and Coach Paul Silas. During their post-season talk, Boozer thought he should have a bigger role in the offense. He didn't want more shots than James, but he believed he should be the second option. Silas thought that center Zydrunas Ilgauskas was the team's second-best offensive player, and that he was the first inside threat. At 7-foot-3, Ilgauskas could make jumpers from medium range or score inside. He was a highly skilled player.

During the conversation, Silas gave Boozer the impression he considered the former Duke star a "role player." Silas denied using that term, but that's how Boozer heard it. The coach talked about rebounding, about creating his own shots by running down court on the fast break or tipping in missed shots from his teammates. Silas was that type of player with Seattle and Boston, and saw Boozer in the same mold. To Silas, it was a compliment to insist Boozer could average 15 points without being a focal point of the offense, and that Boozer playing the role of the muscleman under the boards could help the Cavs one day win a title. Boozer heard it much differently. To him, it was an insult. The coach didn't think he deserved to shoot more. It brought up all the old anger of dropping into the second round of the draft, of having a low-paying contract in his second year. He was beginning to wonder if he'd ever be appreciated and paid what he thought was fair with the Cavs.

On July 8, Paxson was in Portland, Ore., for the funeral of his wife's daughter-in-law. Pelinka called to say that Boozer planned to sign a six-year, $68 million offer sheet with the Jazz. Silas got the message while with family in Oakland, Calif., gathering after the death of his mother, Clara. Gund was on vacation with his family in Canada. Upon hearing the news, he got in his jet and departed for Cleveland to deal with the situation. During the day, Paxson took calls from Gund in his jet in between church and graveside ceremonies at the funeral. Later, the Cavs issued a statement expressing their shock at the events:

To: Cavaliers fans
From: Gordon Gund

I know that last week's developments with respect to Carlos Boozer are a source of extreme disappointment for you. I want to assure you that I feel exactly the same way. Like you, I believed in Carlos.

Several days have now gone by. This has helped me to gain perspective. I hope this letter will do the same for you.

First, Jim Paxson has taken a tremendous amount of criticism in the media for what happened. As the team owner, I made the decision not to pick up the option on Carlos' contract. Any criticism should be directed to me, not to Jim Paxson. I want to be very clear that any fault is mine.

Up until late last week when the trust was broken, I believed in Carlos Boozer, the player, and Carlos Boozer, the person. That is why I tried to do what he said he wanted. We tried to do right by him, by the team and by you in trusting in his repeated insistence that if we showed him respect, he would show respect to us.

Carlos and his agent first approached us in December of 2003, stating his desire for financial security as well as his desire to remain in Cleveland and be a key part of the future of this franchise. He and his agent made it very clear that if we respected them, and provided the security he was looking to gain, he would respect us. Given his record on the court, with the franchise, and in the community, we had every reason to believe his commitment.

Over the course of several months, we had multiple meetings that involved Carlos, his wife and his agent. In our most recent meeting on June 30, Jim Paxson and I told Carlos we had two options. He could play this year on his existing contract and test the market for free agency next year, or we could elect not to exercise the option if we had the understanding with him that as soon as legally possible he would negotiate a contract with us for the maximum we could pay him under league rules.

I told him that as we could not have an agreement at that time given the NBA's Collective Bargaining Agreement, we would have to trust one another's intentions. I said I define trust as his intention to stay in Cleveland and enter into a long term contract with us as soon as possible under the league rules. In that meeting, we were clear with him that he could make more money in the open market a year from now than we could pay him by redoing his contract this year. I told him he needed to understand that and we did not want him to later think we had taken advantage of him. Jim told him, "There are at least seven teams that have cap space right now who will want to pay you more than we can now. We don't want to lose you. Why would we not pick up the option?" Carlos said "Because we'd like long term security and we want to stay in Cleveland." Carlos went on to say that he was happy to be a Cavalier and never indicated any concern with his role on the team or his relationship with Coach Silas.

Carlos, his wife and his agent—all of whom were in that room— knew what our maximum ability would be to pay him. Both Carlos and his wife responded that they wanted financial security now and therefore were anxious to pursue the second option of entering into a long term contract with us as soon as possible and that they would live with any consequences from this decision.

Carlos' agent then said he wanted to go to another room to talk with his client and his wife alone which they did. When they returned, his agent said he had again explained everything to them so that they understood everything involved and said that their thinking had not changed.

Jim Paxson then told him, "We'd like to begin, as soon as permissible, to negotiate an agreement that we can sign on July 14th." Carlos responded, "That's exactly what I want. I want to get this done as quickly as we can."

Over time Carlos had told Jim and me repeatedly, "If you show respect for me, I will show respect for you." So, in the June 30 meeting, I reminded him of that and said, "We are all counting on what you said in earlier meetings and again today." He responded, "That's right and you can trust me on that." I asked if we could all trust each other? Carlos, his wife and agent each responded "Yes." At that point, believing so strongly in Carlos, I said we would not pick up his option. Our intent, as soon as we could do so, was to re-do his contract. The quotes you saw in the media July 1 about his desire to remain here were entirely consistent with what he told us.

In the final analysis, I decided to trust Carlos and show him the respect he asked for. He did not show that trust and respect in return. That's what happened. I wanted you to hear it directly from me. The decision was mine and I take full responsibility.

We currently have no intention of matching Utah's offer to Carlos. In order to match it, and within the restrictions of the NBA's Collective Bargaining Agreement, we would need to make player personnel moves of such a magnitude that it would have significant negative impact on our team moving forward. We are continuing to look at every possible option that will allow us to improve our team and continue to build on the tremendous momentum we have experienced in recent years. More than ever, we are committed to bringing a championship to this city.

Thank you for your continued support of the Cleveland Cavaliers.

Boozer issued his own statement: "There was no commitment, it's unfortunate how it went through the media but I'm really excited to be in the situation I'm in . . . It's against the rules, first of all, to have [a pre-arranged agreement]. I'm not a guy that gives my word and then takes it away, I think I made that clear."

In the end, the Cavs trusted Boozer to keep a promise, although he denies that he ever made a concrete commitment to the Cavs that day. Obviously, the Cavs were sure that he did . . . even the worst run team in the NBA does not allow a talent like Boozer to waltz on to the free agent market when they can keep him for $695,000. But that's how the Cavs must have appeared to much of the NBA, and yes, to LeBron James. Here was James, the Rookie of the Year for a team finally selling out the arena—and his team fails to keep Boozer. It looked like (bad) business as usual for a franchise that had not been in the playoffs for six years, and had five coaches in those six years. This really was Gund's decision to trust Boozer. While Paxson supported it, he is a careful man. It's hard to believe he would have taken that chance alone. Besides, if it was only his call—and the Cavs lost Boozer—it could cost Paxson his job.

"I really believe the Boozer thing was when Gordon first seriously thought about selling the team," said Cavs broadcaster Joe Tait. "It bothered him. Gordon is a very honorable man. I think he sensed the NBA was changing, and he didn't like where it was going."

Three years after losing Boozer, Gund admitted, "It still hurts, just a tremendous disappointment to me. For a short time, it did make me wonder [about staying in the NBA], but it was not the straw that broke the camel's back."

Looking back, Silas wanted it known that his meeting with Boozer had nothing to do with the forward leaving the Cavs. It came down to money. Or as Silas explained, "Gordon had a lot of faith in him. Gordon said if I were to give my word on something, he would believe me. He felt the same way about Boozer . . . I wasn't shocked at all when it happened. Faced with what he was being offered and with what we could offer, it was a heck of a decision. I told our guys to think hard and heavy before doing this. Most of the players empathized with him. He got a lot of money. It was all business."

Terrible business for the Cavs, the kind of business that could cost them LeBron James in a few years when he became a free agent. The Cavs could talk all they wanted about honor and a man's word, but players tend to naturally side with players. If they see a guy getting a better deal elsewhere, they expect him to go—and they don't hold it against the player regardless of what he does to get there. Grab what you can while you can, is the unspoken creed. While Cavs fans took Boozer's name in vain and booed him when he played for Utah in Cleveland, Cavs players talked and joked with him. They didn't care what happened. To them, Boozer is a nice guy who got a lot of money when leaving the Cavs. One day, that might happen to them. James made the usual remarks about a guy "needing to do what was best for his family" and their security.

Even the usually shrewd James could have picked a better way to explain it. Most fans are insulted when they read about a player turning down $40 million for $68 million to "take care of my family." Doesn't $40 million buy enough security? Fans appreciate it more when a player just says, "I wanted the most money I could get, and this was the highest offer."

Paxson knew James was very upset about losing Boozer, and he also knew that putting together a playoff team was critical to keeping James. The thought of all the agony of the losing years to finally get James, and then have him follow Boozer out the door in a few years was terrifying to Paxson. He had to do something, and do it quick.

He had no power forward of consequence. He did have a veteran backup center in 6-foot-11 Tony Battie as depth behind Ilgauskas, and every year several teams are looking for centers. Even a journeymen with aching knees such as Battie, because there are few big men available. It's why the price for Boozer was so high.

"We talked to Karl Malone and wanted to see if he would come out of retirement to play with LeBron," said Paxson. "He'd just had knee surgery, and didn't think he was ready. Karl never did come back and play."

Paxson noticed Orlando had won the lottery and planned to take Dwight Howard with the top pick in the draft. He was a 6-foot-11 high school kid, a power forward. Orlando had Drew Gooden at power forward, and Paxson liked the former Kansas star. Gooden was 6-foot-10, a solid rebounder and decent medium range shooter. He frustrated some coaches because he didn't always grasp the concept of team defense, but Paxson was not about to sweat that detail. He needed size, and needed it now. In some ways, Gooden was a Poor Man's Carlos Boozer. Since he had no Carlos Boozer, he opened talks for Gooden. Orlando was receptive because of Howard arriving. The Magic also wanted a backup center . . . how about Tony Battie, suggested Paxson. Orlando was interested.

"I talked to Paul [Silas] about Gooden," said Paxson. "Paul had talked to some other coaches who had Gooden, and they said he struggled with offenses and defenses. He was cool to the deal. But I said we have no power forward. Orlando is ready to move Gooden somewhere. I'm going to keep talking to them."

Paxson transformed Battie and two future second round picks into Gooden and a young Brazilian who had never played in the NBA.

"I first saw Anderson Varejao playing in the Spanish Cup," said Paxson. "I was scouting another European player, and into the game came this 20-year-old kid with floppy hair. He was a legitimate 6-foot-10, and he could run and jump. He went after every rebound. He was playing behind some older, more experienced European pros. But I knew right away he could play in our league. When we made our draft board for 2004, we had him rated as the 17th best player."

The Cavs had the 10th pick in that draft, selecting Luke Jackson from Oregon. Orlando grabbed Varejao with the 30th pick. So when Paxson was talking trade with Orlando in late July, he wanted two big men—

Gooden and Varejao. He hoped between both of them, the Cavs could at least produce Boozer's 10 rebounds a night. Happy with Howard and ready to hand the power forward spot to their young millionaire, they took Battie and the two second-rounders, shipping Gooden and Varejao to Cleveland. That trade was the best of the Paxson regime, especially since it came during one of the worst months in franchise history. It saved the Cavs from the disaster of Boozer—and possibly helped convince James to sign an extension a few years later. But first, there would be another coach fired, and a new owner.

CHAPTER 14

BRINGING IT TO LIFE

Dan Gilbert buys in

After Gordon Gund finally got The Guy to revive his franchise in LeBron James, he soon went looking for another guy—this one to buy it.

It was David Stern who brought Gordon Gund into the NBA in 1983, and it was Stern who was there to help Gund leave when the Cavaliers owner was ready to sell in 2005.

"Some people thought we might sell during some of the down years [before LeBron James], but I really had no intention of that," said Gund. "I wasn't going to leave the team on a downer. Any owner is a steward for the franchise, which really belongs to the region and the fans. I was determined that when I ever walked away from the Cavs, they'd be in good shape."

The bouncing ping-pong ball during the LeBron Lottery insured that Cavaliers basketball would never be the same, that the gloom and doom attitude along with the swooning attendance was over. The Cavs were about to matter once again, because James gave fans a reason to care.

"I didn't say, 'Great, we've got LeBron, now it's time to sell,'" said Gund. "My goal had always been to win a championship. But as I grew older, the foundation [The Foundation To Fight Blindness which seeks cures and treatments for retinitis pigmentosa and other degenerative eye diseases such as Usher syndrome and macular degeneration] was taking up more and more of my time. We were making tremendous progress. This really was something that would make more of an impact than even the Cavaliers. It wasn't about finding a cure for me.

It may be too late for that. But there are so many more people, and if we could find a cure . . . "

Cavaliers broadcaster Joe Tait considers Gund "an exceptional person." Tait talks about sitting next to Gund at dinner, where someone had to cut up his meat. Gund would feel for the plate, then want to know where to find the food. "Peas at 3 o'clock, potatoes at 6 o'clock, chicken at 9 o'clock," said Tait. "Gordon could then visualize it in his head and watching him eat, you'd never guess he was blind."

Tait said Gund was always a compassionate person, but the blind-ness softened his heart even more—especially to those who had sight problems. It was not uncommon for strangers who had R.P. or some other eye disease to call Gund's office—and he'd call back as soon as possible with encouragement and advice. Gund believed that no matter how many business deals he'd engineer—and there were many great ones—his real call at this stage of his life was his foundation. Stern knew this. The NBA commissioner and Gund had become close friends over the decades, Gund serving on key committees and being one of the people Stern could use as an advisor.

"That's because Gordon Gund is one of the most trustworthy people you'd ever meet," said Tait. "If you tell him something in confidence, it stays in confidence. His blindness also gives him real insight into people and life in general. With Gordon, everything has to go slower, it takes a little more thought. Just walking for him is a challenge and takes planning. He needs to know what is ahead, he has to plan for what may go wrong. He can't just rush off like the rest of us. He'd be a perfect guy for Stern to have as a consultant. One of Gordon's greatest strengths is his patience and ability to listen. He has to listen better than most people, because he can't see."

It's not hard to imagine the hyper-energetic Stern and the thoughtful Gund connecting on a special level, that their relationship may have started with pro basketball and the NBA, then grew into something far more meaningful than how to sell more merchandise, expand to China or secure a labor agreement with the Players Association.

Gund was 63 when the Cavs won the LeBron Lottery. He went into a period of asking himself, "What's really important?" That was es-pecially true because he was convinced the Cavs were in great shape with General Manager Jim Paxson, Coach Paul Silas and James. He realized a title was still several years away, but as Paxson said, "Gordon knew there was good reason to dream that we could win a championship with LeBron."

"I had a conversation with David [Stern] where I mentioned that I was turning 65 and getting more and more involved in the Foundation [to Fight Blindness]," said Gund. "David had recently gotten to know Dan Gilbert. David likes to vet possible owners himself, and he came away with a very positive view of Dan. He said Dan was young, energetic and full of ideas. He said Dan Gilbert would be a good owner, and David's judgment means a lot to me."

In October of 2004, Gund called Paxson into his office, and according to Paxson, Gund said, "I'm only telling you and Mark [Gund Arena CEO Mark Stornes] this, because Mark has to supply the financial information. I don't want Paul Silas to know. I don't want anyone else to know. But within the next month, we are going to Goldman Sachs [the investment firm] to put the team up for sale. I want to find a guy who will be a good owner and keep the team in Cleveland. And I want to make sure the numbers work, or I'm not selling."

So the hunt for the guy with the big bucks—even bigger than what Nike paid for James—was on.

Paxson figured Gund would find someone. LeBron James had made the Cavs a franchise worth owning, and if David Stern were involved, there'd be bidders. Stern considers finding possible buyers for his franchise to be a big part of his job. Just as he recruited Gund to buy the Cavs from Ted Stepien, Stern found someone who was interested in the Cavs—assuming Gund was really sincere about selling.

Dan Gilbert always liked a piece of the action.

He's the son of a military man who later owned a bar. He grew up in Detroit. Nothing came easy, money was tight, the auto industry was starting to fade. In many ways, he's the opposite of Gordon Gund, who came from old money—but then turned it into more money.

Gilbert had no money. His grandfather didn't invent decaffeinated coffee or start Cleveland Trust bank. In life, it is fair to say Gund has hit a home run, especially in the work he's done to battle blindness. But that home run and tremendous charity work was the product of being born on second base. The key was he didn't get picked off. He didn't run in the wrong direction. He didn't become sidetracked, as some sons of wealthy families do. He remained a hard worker, a genuine, humble man who never gave into the disease that stole his sight at the age of 30. But he is a completely different man than Gilbert, who truly is a product of the blue collar, pot-holed streets of Detroit. He knew that there had to be more to life than working 40 hours a week at Ford or Chrysler. More to life than union dues and being subject to the winds of management and economics. More to life than being an average guy, although he had nothing against those who worked with their calloused hands and sore backs.

He just wanted more.

As a kid, Gilbert had sold candy and delivered papers to earn a few bucks. From seeing his father work in a bar, he knew there was money to be made in owning your own business. But it had to be the right business.

"I bought a bunch of Chef Boyardee's pizza," Gilbert said. "I handed out flyers to all the neighbors, saying that my brother and I would make pizzas and deliver them on our bikes. We had a pretty good business going, then the Health Department shut us down. We had violated zoning laws, health laws, you name it. It was my first exposure to regulations."

When Gilbert is with friends and they tell stories from their youth, he mentions this pizza tale. Then he comes up with another from when he was working his way through college.

"I sold and delivered 78 pizzas in one night," he said. "It's still a store record."

It may be, who knows? And who's going to check with the store if the number 78 is true? But anyone knowing Gilbert reasonably well believes he moved 78 pizzas that night. He'd remember things like that. He asks pizza delivery men who come to his house, "What's your record?" He then tells the story of selling 78 pizzas in one night. He calls it "a perfect storm," of people having correct change, answering the doors quickly, traffic lights turning green and the cook whipping them out of the oven at a record pace.

When he was a student at Wayne State, he also tried some real estate. He posted a FOR SALE sign in front of his parents' home. That house wasn't on the market, but it drew some customers, and Gilbert took them to other homes that were for sale. He also became interested in financing and mortgages as he was working his way through law school.

That led him to start Rock Financial, which later became Quicken Loans. In between, Gilbert and his partners sold the company to a corporation called Intuit for $370 million in stock in 1999. The company's name was changed to Quicken Loans, but it struggled under Intuit. They sold it back to Gilbert's company for $64 million in 2002. No wonder he had money ready when David Stern came calling. Stern loves corporate sponsors, and Gilbert was one of the biggest in Detroit. His Rock Financial (as Quicken Loans is still known in Detroit) was a major advertiser in the Palace of Auburn Hills and on the Detroit Pistons radio and television broadcasts. Gilbert had tried to buy the Major League Baseball Milwaukee Brewers in 2004. He was hungry for a piece of big time sports, and Stern sensed it.

"I learned that when you're buying a sports team, you need a legitimate, straight-shooter seller on the other side," said Gilbert. "You have to be so sure of everything, because if a deal of that size becomes public, and it often does, you can end up spinning your wheels."

Gilbert believes he was sucked into a swamp of corporate doubletalk and conflicting agendas. In the end, another group bought the Brewers for about $220 million. News reports say Gilbert offered about $200 million. He claims he missed out on the deal by about $5 million, and perhaps could have indeed bought the team had the sale been handled differently. Stern noticed Gilbert's efforts to purchase the Brewers. He knew that Quicken Loans had become a monster on-line mortgage company since Gilbert bought it back in 2002. He was aware that Gilbert loved pro basketball, as was demonstrated with his interest in the Pistons. He would have been a natural buyer for the Pistons, a hometown Detroit guy. The Pistons were not on the market. But about a three-hour drive away, Gund was interested in selling the Cavaliers with LeBron James to someone who had ties with—or at least a commitment to—Cleveland.

Gilbert had worked with a lawyer named Steve Greenberg, the son of former major league great Hank Greenberg. Steve Greenberg had been a deputy commissioner for Major League Baseball, he also had started the Classic Sports Network, which was later sold to ESPN. He represented Gilbert in the deal to buy the Brewers. He was very connected in the pro sports world.

"Steve called right before the [2004-05] season started and said the Cavaliers were for sale," said Gilbert. "He said the owner of the Cavaliers wanted to deal with one guy. He said he was a straight-shooter. He said, 'They have the whole LeBron thing going, and it's even closer to you than Milwaukee.' I was still bothered by what had happened with the Brewers, but when I heard this, I began to think [not getting the Brewers] could have been a blessing in disguise."

Dan Gilbert was at the Palace of Auburn Hills for the Pistons opener in 2004. So was Stern. They just so happened to end up sitting next to each other, watching the Pistons receive their championship rings. Talk about a great sales pitch without saying a word. You take a driven man like Gilbert, a competitive body builder even in middle age. You put him next to Stern, a master salesman. And since Gilbert has spent much of his life selling ideas and dreams in his various businesses, Stern and Gilbert had a lot in common.

"I never met David Stern before," said Gilbert. "He works for the owners and he wants to keep the value of franchises up. So he'd naturally be interested in [lining up] potential buyers for franchises."

Especially those with cash like Gilbert and in a business such as mortgages which are tightly monitored by the Security and Exchange Commission. Gilbert recalled Stern talking about the big picture NBA, the expansion to China and other markets and on the Internet. It was a sport with a serious salary cap, the kind that gives a team a true home court advantage in free agency. Gilbert knew that if he bought the Cavs, NBA rules meant no team could offer LeBron James more money or more years than Cleveland. The cap fit perfectly for a middle market team such as Cleveland.

"I never really wanted to buy the Pistons," said Gilbert. "Besides, they weren't for sale. But that franchise was already on top. I like the idea of building things, of taking something from the bottom and seeing how high we could go. And it was in Cleveland, a city just begging for a championship. Cleveland is a lot like Detroit. Not only is it close to my home, but it has the same kind of hard-working people. I'd feel very comfortable there. It was close to my company in Livonia, and we could bring our employees down for games on bus rides. It had a lot going for it."

As he watched the Pistons receive their championship rings, Gilbert began to think about what it would be like if that ever happened in Cleveland. A man with a strong sense of sports history, he knew that no major Cleveland pro franchise had won a world title since the 1964 Cleveland Browns. If he could be a part of that . . . he could help build a sports legacy in Cleveland.

"LeBron brought a lot of sex appeal to it," said Gilbert. "But I still think we would have been interested in the Cavaliers without LeBron. Certainly not for $375 million, but I doubt Gordon would have been asking for that kind of money without LeBron. The key for me was taking something that had been down for so long and putting a philosophy and culture into place—believing in your heart and soul you can bring it to life."

Gilbert doesn't care if that sounds trite, it's genuine. The reason Quicken Loans (then Rock Financial) was so successful was the power of ideas, the concept of doing business a different way. Then the reason it floundered after it was sold to Intuit was it lost the basics that made it a mortgage monster. When Gilbert bought it back, he plugged the company and its people into his power, and suddenly, business was better than ever. Gund said he was very impressed with his initial meeting with Gilbert. The two men talked business, Gund drawing out Gilbert about how he built Quicken Loans and how he thought business should be done.

"We had a lot of people checking on Dan and his business," said Gund. "We knew that he had it [the money] to make a deal. But I wanted to know why he wanted the team. I wanted to make sure he'd be the right guy for Cleveland. I could tell he was bright, a quick study and he was very interested in other people. I sensed he could be the right guy for the franchise."

Gund said that he had spoken to possible buyers before, "but they didn't have what was needed. I didn't want to sell to someone who'd run it on a shoe string, or have a group of nine owners like they did in New Jersey for a while. If I were going to sell, it was going to be to someone who had a clear controlling interest as owner, so there would be no doubt who was in charge. It also would be someone who had the resources so we make sure we can keep LeBron."

Gund understood how hard it was to Get The Guy who'd change the course of the franchise on the court. But the next crucial step was retaining him, and strong ownership was the key.

"Part of me didn't want to sell," said Gund. "I didn't want to be a quitter before the job [a championship] was done. We had put a lot of money into it to get to this point. I thought I had a strong person in Jim [Paxson] to run it. But I also knew that if I found the right guy, it was time to sell."

The man who wanted the Cavs believes the most important thing you have is time.

"I know of people who have made a million dollars, lost it, then made it back," said Gilbert. "You can have a car stolen and replace it. You can replace most things, but not time. Once time is gone, it's gone."

Gilbert was speaking to a group of of new employees at his Quicken Loans office as he does every few months.

While his thoughts on time might not be entirely original, it truly bothers him that most of us don't cherish time, that we spend more time thinking about how to spend money than we do about how best to use time. Time can create wealth, it can strengthen relationships, it can make us smarter or it can be utterly wasted.

Most of the people in the room were between the ages of 20 and 40, slightly more women than men. Quicken Loans is located in Livonia, a Detroit suburb. It's in an enormous four-story building, with bright lights, plush carpets and few closed-in offices. During his talk to the new employees, many were surprised that Gilbert was spending his time on this subject rather than just droning about how better to sell a mortgage.

In fact, during his three segments—about five hours—he rarely mentioned mortgages at all. Instead, he talked about what he believes matters most in business and life.

He is obsessive about communication. On the three huge screens

in the conference room where he speaks appeared these words: WE
RETURN ALL PHONE CALLS TO EVERYONE EVERY TIME. If you
don't do it quickly, the training guide warns in red capital letters: YOU
CANNOT AND WILL NOT WORK HERE ANYMORE. Gilbert says, WE
WILL FIND YOU AND ROOT YOU OUT.

Quicken Loans is booming, hiring about 200 people every few
months. It has grown from 1,666 employees in 2003 to 2,227 in 2004
to 3,200 in 2005 to 3,944 in 2007. *Fortune* magazine rated it among the
top 15 places to work from 2003 to 2007. *Computerworld* magazine
ranked it No. 1 for companies in the tech industry. There also is turn-
over. The rewards for production are high, but not everyone will buy
into "The World According To Dan." You can find blogs on the Internet
from unhappy former Quicken Loans employees, who felt unappre-
ciated and couldn't deal with the demands of the company. Some
claimed they were on the verge of nervous breakdowns before they
quit or were fired. There also are numerous success stories—people
who struggled in different businesses and suddenly were inspired and
empowered when they joined Quicken Loans.

As you walk through the second floor of the four-story facility, you
see some sales people in front of computers, others pacing as they talk
on headsets. Giant screens keep track of each call, the sales person,
the time of the call and the eventual outcome.

"Supervisors"—Gilbert hates that word, preferring "team leaders"—
sometimes listen in. Scoreboards record results. It's not cutthroat, but
it is competitive. Regardless of your stance about online mortgages,
creative sales techniques and hip, non-corporate-culture-type companies where employees can wear nice jeans, sweatshirts and tennis
shoes—much of what Gilbert is doing works. During the interview
process, possible Quicken applicants are sometimes asked, "What are
the three worst things that happened to you?" The point is not to dig
up dirt from the past but to discover how people dealt with personal
setbacks. Did they get snared in the blame game?

"We hired two women in their early 50s, both had just been through
a tough divorce," said Gilbert. "They had a lot in common, same basic
level of education. They worked in the same branch, same department,
under the same leader. One became one of our top mortgage brokers,
the other became very bitter and left the company. I asked myself
what was the difference? One saw herself as a victim. You sometimes

can tell when people often say something always happens to them or people never appreciate them. It's hard to change that attitude."

During his presentation, Gilbert does not tell his business story—an inspiring tale. He doesn't talk about starting the company with the $5,000 he says he made selling pizzas. He was 22 years old when the business was born in 1985. It was a basic mortgage company called Rock Financial. In 1996, he decided the future was the Internet and began with 16 people in a Web center. Nor does he mention that he's worth close to $1 billion and is on the Forbes 400 list of the richest people in America. He doesn't want the company to be about him, or even about how much money you can make working for Quicken Loans. (The average mortgage banker pockets about $80,000 annually from sales. Some are above $300,000.)

"A few years ago, we had a labor shortage," he said. "We were working a lot of hours, and I had catered lunches and dinners brought in for our employees so they could use their time better. Eat well at the office, if they chose to. It cost about $100,000 a month for several months, but it made us several million each month. It saved time, which created wealth."

His company has "The Guy." It's a place to call when something goes wrong, and you can get an answer. Computer broken? Supplies needed? Something confusing about a pending sale? "Don't call a committee meeting," Gilbert said. "Don't wait to try and figure out what 'they' say you should do. Call The Guy." The Guy might be a woman. It's actually a group of people whose sole purpose is to keep the company running smoothly, to help employees find answers. Gilbert believes companies waste so much time because they don't have people assigned to find answers for those who are on the front lines of sales and other positions.

"You call The Guy with a question," he said. "The Guy calls you back."

Gilbert is about 5-foot-7, 180 pounds. He is a serious weight lifter, and his upper body shows it. His company is informal—very few suits and ties. Gilbert often wears a casual sweater and corduroy pants. To the new employees, he presented a memo from another company chastising people in the office for giving each other high-fives when closing a sale. He was stunned that time was spent on such trivia.

While Gilbert grew up in Detroit, he sees himself as a Midwestern boy on his own, a little like rocker Bob Seger, who came from Detroit and made a national name for himself yet still lives in Michigan. That's part of the reason why that when Gilbert bought the Cavs, he opened a Quicken Loans office in Cleveland.

"Cleveland feels like home to me," he said. "This is a great part of the country. I like the people; I like the town."

Not long after that championship ring ceremony at the Palace of Auburn Hills, Gilbert and his business partners began serious negotiations to purchase the Cavs. On the other side of the table was Cavs Vice Chairman John Graham, a large, kind man—as long as you aren't making a business deal with him. Gilbert said Gund and Graham were two of the toughest negotiators he's ever encountered. Graham is straight talking and utterly honest, but he knows when he's dealing from a position of strength and he's not about to bend on much. His job is to make the best deals for Gund, and he does it better than anyone.

The price would be $375 million—stunningly high for a team in Cleveland. And Gund would retain 15 percent of the ownership.

Naturally, it was Gund's hand and guidance that was behind Graham. He was like the offensive coordinator in the football press box, calling down the plays to the quarterback—who puts them into action on the field of play, making the appropriate adjustments in the heat of battle.

"We had no problem letting Gordon keep 15 percent," said Gilbert. "He's a good man, and he wanted to keep a hand in the team. But we have controlling interest, that was the key. We started talking in November and we signed the deal on January 2, 2005. It was quick because Gordon wanted it that way. As far as I know, there were no other bidders. He either was going to make a deal with us or keep the team."

Or as Gund said, "I have no say in running the team, nor should I. There should only be one majority owner. My goal was to sell the franchise when it was in good shape—and it was. And to sell it to a guy committed to Cleveland, and Dan Gilbert is."

This was probably the first time Gilbert has been seriously accused of overpaying for a business proposition.

"I see it differently," he said. "To me, NBA franchises are like pieces of art. There are only 30 of them. They aren't always on the market, especially a franchise that would have been such a natural fit for us as was Cleveland. If you just looked at the Cavaliers in terms of revenues, profits and balance sheets—and you paid this amount for it—people would say, 'You're insane! You're nuts.' But if you look at the tentacles, the impact on our other ventures, it makes tremendous sense. We now have opened a Cleveland office [of Quicken Loans] and that's tremendously successful. Our employees love it that we're associated with the Cavs and they can come to games—that helps us attract and keep better people. There are a lot of non-profit things that can be done with pro sports. It brings an unbelievable amount of excitement."

And exposure.

When a person wants a mortgage, Gilbert's goal is for them to immediately think of Quicken Loans. The arena is named after Quicken Loans. So every time the Cavs play a home game, Quicken Loans Arena is mentioned in newspapers and radio and television. At the games, Quicken Loans is advertised. He wants to make "mortgages" and "Quicken Loans" one and the same, much as people say "Kleenex" when they want paper tissue to blow their nose. The brand name becomes the name—and how can you put a price on that?

Gilbert was a smart guy in business, a genius when it came to marketing mortgages. But when it came to basketball. he found out the hard way that he had a lot to learn.

CHAPTER 15

"YOU HAVE TO TAKE THE ROAST OUT OF THE OVEN"

Dan Gilbert learns the hard way

One of Dan Gilbert's "Isms" is, "You have to take the roast out of the oven."

It's in the manual that he hands to new Quicken Loans employees. It continues: "Wrap it up. Finish the job. Execute! Over-analyzing can kill an idea and possibly make you miss an opportunity."

When the deal to purchase the Cavaliers was signed and approved by the NBA in early March of 2005, Gilbert was ready to move.

"It wasn't long that I was hearing from friends around the league that Gilbert and his people were asking about me and the trades we made," said Paxson. "They were talking to Maverick Carter and some of LeBron's other people. I was getting a bad feeling."

As this story unfolds, keep in mind that everyone has their own version of what happened. Remember that Paxson was still dealing with his wife's major cancer problems. His reputation had been battered by all the losing and the moves he made to put the team in position to draft LeBron James. It also was hurt by Carlos Boozer's departure, despite the fact that Gordon Gund made the final decision on that and issued an official statement to prove it. Paxson knew that some of his draft choices had flopped. His best pick was Andre Miller, but he was traded for Darius Miles when the Cavs made the decision to sink in the standings in the hopes of climbing to the top of the draft lottery. His next best draft selection was Boozer, and he was gone, too. His relationship with Paul Silas also was showing strain.

Gilbert was aware of this not long after he began to negotiate to buy the Cavaliers. Yes, LeBron James was the key guy. But if he had the wrong management team in place, Gilbert feared he would not have James for long.

Another of his "Isms" reads: "Time, not money, is the scarcest commodity of all. It can never be replaced. What will you choose to do with the 31,536,000 seconds you get each year?"

Gilbert sensed the Cavaliers were wasting time, especially with some of the internal struggles between Paxson and Silas.

Paxson said the problems with Silas began after the season when Gordon Gund set up a meeting at his home with Silas and Paxson. Paxson said it was a review of the season, and they also were going to give Silas a bonus check of $1 million. It was part of his four-year, $16 million deal. If his team won at least 34 games in the first season—doubling the previous victory total—he'd receive the extra $1 million in addition to his $4 million base pay for that season. The team was 35-47, so Silas earned it. Paxson said most of the meeting was positive, but Paxson was in favor of replacing assistant coach Bob Donewald Jr. This is always a touchy area, as head coaches like to pick their own staff—especially a veteran head coach such as Silas. He had hired former Golden State assistant Mark Osowski, his son Stephen Silas (who had been with Silas in New Orleans) and Donewald. Paxson allowed Silas to name his own staff, not wanting to do anything that would stop Silas from taking the Cavs job.

But now, Paxson believed Osowski was the strongest member of the coaching staff, but Donewald "always had Paul's ear."

Even if Silas agreed, he was not about to give in. It was a battle over territory.

"I said we had to get rid of Bob [Donewald] and we had a pretty heated discussion," said Paxson. "In the end, he agreed."

Suddenly, the final season meeting that was supposed to be a reward for Silas with the bonus check ended with the coach defensive, the general manager probably picking the wrong time to bring up Donewald. In the big picture, Donewald was barely a dot on the landscape. That issue could have been dealt with later. In his bestselling book *The 7 Habits of Highly Effective People*, author Stephen Covey writes about how we need to make sure the "Main Thing" remains the

"Main Thing." Don't get distracted, don't lose focus. Don't let little things—like the Donewald issue—become the main thing. It's harder than it sounds, because humans are just that—human. You take two former NBA players in Paxson and Silas who are very good at what they do and known for their work ethic and preparation. Add in the pressure of a very public, extremely scrutinized job and the need for both of them to succeed. There will be clashes. There also is a natural conflict between the general manager and coach in most organizations. The general manager picks the players, the coach takes those players and is supposed to transform them into a winner. On many teams, the general manager believes the coach is not getting the most out of the players. The coach believes the general manager has overrated the players. That makes sense, since he drafted or traded for them. The coach thinks the problem isn't Xs and Os, it's that he (the coach) needs more talent than he's been handed by the general manager. The general manager thinks the coach could help the players he has flourish with more minutes or tactical adjustments.

Paxson said there were times when Silas seemed "stubborn about looking at new possibilities. I wasn't trying to coach for him. Maybe these meetings were hard for him because of what happened [being fired] in New Orleans. Maybe he had a trust issue. I had issues at home [his wife's cancer]. It was a hard time for both of us."

Coaching is more than just knowing Xs and Os. It's keeping players somewhat content and buying into your vision of the team. It's making sure that while they may not like your decisions, they can trust you to be honest with them when they want to know why they have a certain role on the team. For a general manager, it's not just finding the best talent, it's discovering which talented players can mesh together with the current roster and coach to improve the team. For an owner, it's making sure his coach and general manager aren't sabotaged by the torpedoes of insecurity that are a part of these jobs where so many are fired each year. Gund has said that one of the roles of an owner is to intervene and play peacemaker.

Paxson said there were times when "Paul thought we were telling him that he didn't do a good job, and that wasn't true."

It's so easy for a coach to take suggestions as criticism, especially when it comes from the general manager during a losing streak. There were clouds of disappointment in the air of that meeting as the Cavs just missed the playoffs by a single game. Any coach, general manager or player looks back to find one game, one decision, one play that could have made a difference. The Cavs really wanted James to get a taste of playoffs as a rookie, and they also knew it would have been another signal to the fans and media that the franchise indeed had made a major turnaround.

Losing can bring out the worst in everyone. Silas had been wounded by being fired after doing a good job in New Orleans, sensing that not everyone in the Hornet organization had supported him. Paxson loves to talk basketball, and he would meet with Silas weekly, discussing such topics as how to defend the pick-and-roll, which was a problem for the Cavs the first year. Silas took this as criticism. Paxson considered it brainstorming. Because he had been fired twice as a head coach—early in his career with the Los Angeles Clippers and later with the Hornets—Silas was sensitive to criticism, especially from his bosses.

Then came the Boozer fiasco, followed by Paxson trading Tony Battie and a pair of second-round draft choices to Orlando for Anderson Varejao and Drew Gooden. Silas knew nothing of Varejao, who had averaged 7.7 points and 5.1 rebounds coming off the bench for Barcelona in the Euroleague. Paxson had scouted Varejao intensely, and loved the 6-foot-10 forward's relentless defense, hustle and commitment to rebounding. To Silas, it sounded like this 21-year-old was a project. Silas did know Gooden, and word around the league was that the power forward was immature and struggled with defense. He was the fourth pick out of Kansas in 2002 by Memphis, but he was traded to Orlando in the middle of his rookie year. Gooden averaged 11.6 points and 6.5 rebounds.

To Silas, it seemed that neither could come close to replacing Boozer.

To Paxson, it was the best he could do, given the urgency to find someone before the season to play power forward.

To the credit of Silas, he put together a solid team to start the 2004–05 season, and Gooden credits Silas with reviving his career.

Paxson had also traded for Eric Snow, now giving Silas two point guards where a year ago there were none. While there was some strain between Jeff McInnis and Snow, Silas was able to juggle that reasonably well for a while. There was an early-season blowup when Silas was upset with Snow's attitude, and threw the veteran guard off the bench in the middle of a game. It seemed like shooting an ant with an elephant gun, or at least that's how Silas' critics saw it. Snow was not standing up or gesturing—things that would appear as open rebellion against the coach. Snow also is considered one of the classiest players in the NBA, a man often honored for his civic duty. His other coaches loved his unselfishness and defensive presence. That's why Paxson traded for him, especially with McInnis being known for his volatility. But Silas thought Snow was ignoring his authority and had a bad attitude that night. Silas believed he was just keeping order and demanding respect, that it was no different than he'd do with any other player. Nor did he hold any grudge against Snow and it was common for him to play Snow in clutch situations.

The Cavs began the season at 12-6, and they were 31-24 when Gilbert officially took over the team on March 1, 2005.

The relationship between Paxson and Silas remained touchy. Making it worse was Gund's preoccupation with the pending sale to Gilbert. Gund had always been a favorite of both men, a stabilizer in their relationship. Silas and Paxson also were very aware that a new owner might want to bring in his own management team. That often happens in pro sports. Then came a time when Paxson refused to trade Gooden to the New York Knicks as part of a deal for Kurt Thomas. Silas wanted to make the trade, but Thomas had signed a huge contract and Paxson believed taking on all the money would just clog up the salary cap. He also thought Gooden, averaging 14.4 points and 9.2 rebounds, was playing well, despite his occasional lapses on defense. In fact, Gooden was having the best season of his young career, responding well to Silas.

So when Gilbert assumed ownership, he encountered a strange situation. The Cavs were off to one of their best starts in seven seasons and they had James playing better than ever.

"But it was completely dysfunctional," said Gilbert. "There was no trust. The GM and the coach didn't talk to each other. I'm mean, literally, they didn't talk to each other. To me, it seemed insane. I had a 45-minute talk with Paul Silas, and I thought it was pretty good. Because it was Paul Silas, I was even walking on eggs some. He gets out of that meeting and tells people that I was going to fire him."

Gilbert said he was receiving e-mails from players about problems with the team and Silas. One veteran who had been with several teams, "a credible guy in the league," told Gilbert that he had never been in "such a screwed up situation." He said he talked to James, who didn't seem very happy with the situation either—but he also didn't criticize anyone. Of course, when players sense a coach is in some trouble, the critics do come out.

Remember, everyone has their own version of events.

Paxson said while the relationship with Silas was difficult, he could live with it. Besides, the team was winning. Silas believes had Gund remained in charge, everything would have worked out. Paxson agrees. Gund says he still has tremendous respect for both men. But all of that is irrelevant, because Gund was no longer the majority owner. Within a few days after Gilbert became owner, there were rumors that Gilbert or at least someone in his group didn't think Silas was a good coach. Some members of the local media heard it, and no doubt, Silas did, too. That's why the meeting between the new owner and coach probably went so poorly. Silas wasn't about to trust anything that was said. Unlike now, when Gilbert makes sure that his voice is the one voice of the organization, it seemed his associates were talking and calling people around the NBA, wanting opinions on the Cavaliers. The NBA often is fueled by gossip and conspiracy theories, and they were flying in early March, especially when that three-game winning streak was immediately followed by a the Cavs losing five of six.

"Dan was chomping at the bit and had done a lot of due diligence on myself and the coaches," said Paxson. "I had a meeting at Quicken Loans with Dan and some of his people. They were asking questions like, 'Why can't we win a championship now?' We were in a conference room with all of Dan's 'Isms' on the board. Some of the people were asking me why we couldn't trade for a guy like Baron Davis so 'we could win a championship right now.' I told them that Davis is not a good fit, that he has to have the ball a lot—and we wanted LeBron to have the ball. Davis also had a bad back, and a huge contract. Then they wanted to get some other players. It went on a long time. [Cavaliers legal counsel] Dick Watson was in the meeting, too. Afterwards, he told me that I had handled it fine. He said if Wayne Embry had been in that meeting, he would have flipped the table over. Looking back, maybe I should have."

Paxson talked about another meeting where Gilbert's associates "had a huge board with names of players and their salaries, and wanted to know how we could get these guys. There were eight people in the room, and some of them I didn't know very well. One of them wanted to know if we fired Silas, could we get Pat Riley."

Another of Gilbert's "Isms" reads: "It's not about WHO is right, it's about WHAT is right. It's doesn't matter where ideas come from in our family, what matters is the idea is the right ideas. In our flat organization, great input and ideas can come from everywhere. Egos (or lack thereof) are checked at the door. If the Chairman and CEO are wrong and the 'new guy' is right, then the new guy's idea or point is followed."

Gilbert also says, "Failure *is* an option. *Not trying* is failure."

Paxson sensed that some around Gilbert wondered if he was indeed trying hard enough to win right now, if he had examined every angle and possibility to improve the team. These people didn't know Paxson, who was obsessed with making the Cavaliers better. You can question his judgment and moves, but not his effort and homework. Sessions such as those attended by Paxson often are very productive in a progressive, quick moving company such as Quicken Loans. Gilbert becomes sincerely excited when he receives an e-mail from a low level employee with what he'd call a "high level" idea or way of doing business. One of Gilbert's strengths is collecting ideas, sorting through the best, using an open mind to integrate them into his company—not caring who submitted the idea. While anyone can e-mail a boss at Quicken Loans with an idea, it's impractical for an NBA general manager to sort through thoughts and concepts from employees, fans and fantasy league types. Paxson knew the Cavs were not close to a championship caliber team. The goal for the season was to make the playoffs, perhaps win a round so the team could gain some post-season experience, then continue to add talent over the summer. You don't go from winning 17 games to competing for an NBA title in two years, regardless of how gifted James might be. Paxson tried explaining that, over and over.

It's also what Gordon Gund told Gilbert at the press conference where the team changed hands—be patient.

Gilbert wanted to tug the roast out of the oven, replace his coach now. He said he was receiving e-mails from players complaining about Silas. The relationship between his two top basketball men really worried him. Gilbert could sense the playoffs slipping away.

"I told Dan to keep things in place [with Silas and Paxson], but it was not my decision," said Gund. "Paul was very nervous about the ownership change. I learned over the years that rarely does changing coaches in the middle of a season help. If you let a coach go like that, it's hard to hold things together."

Paxson said about a week after becoming owner, Gilbert wanted to fire Silas. He'd replace Silas with Brendan Malone, who had joined the staff as an assistant that season. Malone had been a long-time Detroit assistant coach, and also been a head coach in Toronto.

"I gave them a two-page memo on why we shouldn't make a change," said Paxson. "The success rate of interim coaches is terrible and some other reasons. I fought for him for two weeks."

The problem was more than just losing, Silas began to coach like a guy who sensed he was about to lose his job. He was uptight. His substitution patterns changed dramatically, as he played his starters (especially James) huge minutes. One game, James scored 56 points on 18-of-36 shooting when the Cavs lost 105-98 at Toronto. The offense had degenerated into throwing the ball to James, with his four teammates watching him as he jacked up shots trying desperately to hold things together. Silas seemed unable to bring the passion to the team that they showed early in the season. He was very concerned about his own future. That loss in Toronto was the ninth in 12 games. Gilbert decided to replace Silas. It was only three weeks after he became owner, and the Cavs were 34-30.

"During that game, I got a message on my BlackBerry that they wanted to fire Paul," said Paxson. "The next day, we called Paul in. It was Dan and myself. I told Paul that he was fired. Dan thanked him, and it was over in five minutes."

"I thought it was a colossal mistake when they fired Silas," said Cavs broadcaster Joe Tait. "We needed a firm, strong hand and Paul was that. He was probably a little too tough for some of our modern gladiators, but he was a solid, solid coach. One of the issues was Jeff McInnis. Silas had had it up to his ears with McInnis, and he told McInnis, 'As long as I'm coaching this team, you'll never play for me again.' I saw it at the airport, Silas put McInnis right up to the wall. Not hitting him, but giving him a piece of his mind. He later told the coaches, 'If this costs me my job, so be it.' The next day, he was gone."

Obviously, it was more than Jeff McInnis that cost Silas his job. He believed he'd be fired, and then coached like a man preoccupied with those thoughts. Because he was not getting along with Paxson, he felt little support from the front office. Paxson had concerns of his own, as he knew Gilbert wasn't sold on him as a general manager, either.

At this point, Gilbert was about to learn some very painful lessons.

It began with interim coaches, who are viewed by the players like substitute teachers. In league where the average coach survives barely three years with a team, players often pay too little attention to what the full-time coach has to say. But when they know the guy is just keeping the seat warm until the end of the season—they may play hard, but they don't fully buy into what the interim coach is selling. Why should they? The next year someone else will have the job. That's why Lawrence Frank, Stan Van Gundy, Mike D'Antoni and Rudy Tom-janovich are the only interim coaches since 1990 to have any degree of success. Yes, there have been coaches such as George Karl and Hubie Brown who joined a team during the season and turned the losing around—but they were big names armed with long-term contracts. They had about as much security as a coach can in the NBA. Malone had nothing like that. Like Silas before him, he had reason to wonder if he would be in the same job next year.

Silas is a popular, respected figure in the NBA and with the media. From the outside, the firing seemed outrageous. Silas took over a team that was 17-65. He took it to 35-47 the first season, and was 34-30 when fired. What did he do wrong? Who did Dan Gilbert think he was, Red Auerbach?

Gilbert said the first NBA owner to sincerely reach out to him was Mark Cuban of the Dallas Mavericks. Both are middle-aged, self-made, highly-intelligent and driven men. They built their business empires by defying conventional thinking. One of the first messages Cuban sent Gilbert was, "Go with your instincts, don't just listen to the old guard."

But Cuban has never fired a coach at mid-season, and has had only two coaches since 2000—Don Nelson and Avery Johnson. For all his volatility, Cuban realized stability is a key when it comes to coaches.

Rumors whirled. Gilbert was sending notes to the bench telling Silas what to do—not true whatsoever. He was letting LeBron's mother travel on a private jet. When that was reported, Gilbert had not yet even met Gloria James. He was going to fire Paxson the day after Silas was fired. Not true. At least not until the end of the season. Then there were reports that Larry Brown—destined to be fired in Detroit—would come to Cleveland as general manager, coach or perhaps both. All of this during the final weeks of the season when the Cavs should have been focused on making the playoffs.

"The Larry Brown thing was the most overblown thing I've ever heard of," said Gilbert. "I think it was his people reaching out to us, saying Larry had some physical problems and while he'd like to coach, he may not be able to . . . and they wanted to talk to us about [a front office job] after the season . . . we said we'd talk after the season, and that was it."

Then came a news report that Gilbert had been arrested in 1981 for helping to run a gambling ring while a student at Michigan State. He was fined, placed on probation and given 100 hours of community service. The criminal charges have since been erased from his record.

"I was shocked when that came out," said Gilbert. "I was like 18 or 19 years old. A bunch of us kids had those Sunday pool football sheets, and about 30 guys put money in it. One kid lost like 200 bucks and he goes and tells his dad. His dad calls the state police, and they came in. . . . we had this little blue book where we kept track of the numbers of what each kid owed, no one even exchanged money. They brought it in and the judge said, 'Stay out of trouble for three or six months' or whatever, and they dismissed it. . . . some 22 years later, it came out. I couldn't believe it. David Stern knew about it."

According to a report in the *Lansing Journal*, Gilbert and three other students had a ring where $114,000 was handled. Gilbert said that number was incredibly inflated. His main point is that was in 1981, and this was 2005. He had never been in any legal trouble, and his mortgage company means he has to run a solid business because it's regulated by 50 state regulators.

But the reports just fueled skepticism and criticism. And the biggest worry was: *LeBron is going to look at all this and get out of here as fast as he can!*

Fans feared Gilbert was some cocky guy from Detroit who thought he knew more than the basketball people, and he was going to mess up a franchise that finally seemed to be straightening out. More than a few fans were convinced he actually planned to move the team. Paranoia from losing the Browns to Baltimore after the 1995 season was still alive in some minds. The moving speculation was ridiculous. Gilbert was from Detroit, and that city already had a team. It would make no sense for him to move to Oklahoma City or somewhere else. Cleveland was the next best thing to Detroit for him, because it was so close to his home. Also, the Cavs signed a very tight lease tying them to Gund Arena.

But for the rest, who knew what would happen?

As veteran broadcaster Joe Tait said, "I didn't trust Dan and I didn't like him when he first arrived because I didn't know him. The few brief times we did talk, I didn't get a good feel for him. Later, my opinion changed dramatically."

That's probably what most fans thought about Gilbert's first few stormy months.

The season ended with the Cavs missing the playoffs on the final night. They won their last game in Toronto, but that wasn't enough as they also needed New Jersey to lose to Boston. The Nets won. The next day, Paxson was fired, as was Malone, who had a decent 8-10 record for an interim coach.

"I thanked Dan when he fired me, because I knew it was coming and he handled it well," said Paxson. "I put together a short list of coaches for him. I set up a meeting with [former Minnesota coach] Flip Saunders and his agent, Mark Termini. I thought Flip was an excellent coach, and advised Dan to just get him hired and move forward. Flip had coached Kevin Garnett in Minnesota. He was a Cleveland guy. I thought he'd relate well to LeBron and help us get LeBron to sign an extension when the time came. Flip is a good offensive coach, and he's OK on defense. Dan didn't seem to like Flip very much. They had dreams of Larry Brown and Pat Riley. I even put in a call to Riley, who was not coaching the Heat but in their front office at the time. Pat had a deal as a part owner that was very lucrative. He was gracious, but not interested. Look, they wanted their own guys. Now, I can understand that."

Gilbert said it would have been wiser just to stick with Silas until the end of the season. But he was conflicted because "I believed from Day One that we needed to make a clean sweep . . . Jim Paxson is a nice guy, but he just wasn't our kind of guy."

Gilbert added that he would have fired both men even if the team had made the playoffs. He wanted to start fresh with his own people. That may sound harsh, but it's what most new owners do in pro sports. Gilbert has a list that he gives to all Quicken Loans employees of "21 Things Dan Gilbert Has Learned in 21 Years." On that list, No. 4 reads: "Some people will NEVER get it. Get them out of your team, your club, house, life, etc. You both will be happier."

Right or wrong, he was convinced Paxson and Silas would never get his way of doing business. No. 10 on the list reads: "Nothing great and long lasting is built overnight, but you MUST take the first step NOW." That's what he did by firing them, despite not really being sure what he'd do next.

But that also doesn't dismiss the fact that Silas and Paxson did far more right than wrong in Cleveland.

"I thought Jim Paxson did a great job when you consider what he was supposed to do," said Joe Tait. "He first came in to cut payroll. Getting rid of Shawn Kemp, I still think he must have had a mask and a gun to get that done. I've been around the league for 37 years and I've seen it time and time again where a GM comes in to create a bad team in order to get the guy so you can have a good team—and he does it. But then he's not around when the team does start to win. Jim created lots of salary cap room that helped them put together the team that went to the NBA Finals [in 2007]. He'll never get the credit he deserves."

Paxson left the Cavs with $28 million room on the salary cap to sign free agents. His trade for Gooden and Varejao was excellent. He picked up Sasha Pavlovic for a first-rounder, and Pavlovic was a key player when the Cavs won the 2007 Eastern Conference title. His addition of Eric Snow was a positive.

He missed terribly, trading a 2007 first-rounder for Jiri Welsch, and his draft record was spotty—especially after the loss of Boozer. But overall, he put the Cavs in position to get LeBron James, and then manipulated the salary cap so the team could sign some significant free agents.

As for Silas, he did bring stability and credibility that first season. He gave the fans a sense of confidence, knowing an experienced coach was on the bench to help James during his rookie season. Would Paxson and Silas have led the Cavs to the Eastern Conference title in

2007? Their relationship was deteriorating, but perhaps Gund could have held it together. Who knows? But without Gund, it never would have worked.

"I believe the team would have made the playoffs and done OK in the post season [if there were no changes]," said Gund. "Missing the playoffs and the criticism was good for Dan because it forced him to learn some things quickly, and he did. I told him to work through the pros, let them make the decisions—then hold them accountable. It takes time for players, coaches and the general manager to get to know each other. If there is stability, things will improve—assuming you have the right people."

Gund said it was crucial for Gilbert to deal with his general manager, "not allow his friends to give their ideas." He said basketball is different than other businesses, and you can't transfer some concepts from business to pro basketball. And just because you built a successful business doesn't automatically make you a good NBA owner. He stressed to Gilbert to keep information to himself, "because everything you talk to someone about may end up in print. It can come back on you adversely and impact your team, making it tough on the franchise."

Gilbert did indeed learn that lesson, as he cut down on the number of interviews he did—and was very careful about what he said, especially when it came to questions about players, coaches and basketball issues.

"What I see in Dan is a quick study," said Gund. "For example, he changed some of the ways we did things on the business side of the operation, but he kept our key people in place—because they are good people. That said a lot for Dan. He didn't make changes just to make changes. I was impressed by that. While what happened that first season really hurt Dan, it showed him what he needed to do to become a good owner. "

And to make sure LeBron James didn't reject a chance to sign a contract extension in the summer of 2006. While Paxson's job was to get The Guy, Gilbert had to find the right people so that the Cavs could keep The Guy in Cleveland.

CHAPTER 16

"A CHANCE TO DO SOMETHING SPECIAL"

Danny Ferry to the rescue

Before Dan Gilbert bought the Cavaliers, he thought he knew what it meant to be a general manager.

"Every year, you have draft pick, you maybe make a trade, maybe sign a free agent," he said. "And every five years, you maybe hire a coach."

How hard could it be, he wondered.

Then he stumbled into the Cavaliers in a playoff run and discovered how little he really knew about basketball. It was a humbling experience for a man who not only turned Quicken Loans into a mortgage monster, but has a law degree from Wayne State, is a member of the Michigan Bar and won the 1999 "Entrepreneur of the Year" award from Ernst and Young. He also was a Detroit Pistons season ticket holder and one of the franchise's biggest corporate sponsors. He had a lot of friends around the NBA. In a sense, he should have known better. But sometimes, a bright guy can know just enough to be really wrong.

As the Cavaliers collapsed around him, Gilbert was hammered in the media for being a meddler who seemed to believe he was smarter about basketball than former star players such as Jim Paxson and Paul Silas. No one in Cleveland cared that Quicken Loans has consistently been named one of the nation's best places to work by *Fortune* magazine and *Computerworld*, or that he is considered one of the savviest businessmen in America.

Selling more online mortgages than anyone else doesn't win a single NBA game, or inspire confidence from any Cavaliers ticket holder. Gilbert came across as an interloper from Michigan who not only cost the team a playoff berth, but perhaps a chance to re-sign LeBron James.

For nearly two months after the season, he had one basketball man in place—relentless Mark Warkentein. He had been Paxson's top assistant, and was an able scout with lots of NBA contacts. He actually would have been a reasonable choice to be general manager, but Gilbert wanted his own people. In the meantime, Warkentein was staying at the downtown Cleveland Residence Inn—never a sign of security.

Warkentein was pushing Gilbert to hire Flip Saunders as coach. He was stressing that the Cavs needed to keep free agent center Zydrunas Ilgauskas. It seemed Gilbert's people had little interest in Ilgauskas. They wanted a defensive presence such as the Pistons' Ben Wallace. It's easy to say, "We need a Ben Wallace-type center." It's much harder to find one when Wallace is already in Detroit. Warkentein was stressing that Ilgauskas had some flaws, but at 7-foot-3 with a nice medium range jumper and a knack for tipping in offensive rebounds, he was a Top 10 NBA center. He was the kind of player, like Brad Daugherty, who would not be truly missed until he was gone.

But no one thought Warkentein would survive. No one knew where Gilbert would find a general manager, and for a while, neither did Gilbert.

"I was naive about the whole thing," he admitted.

He realized that he had to get the right guys . . . the right general manager . . . the right coach.

Then he had to take the advice of Gordon Gund and others, namely, to get out of the way and let them do their jobs. Give them what they needed. Don't micromanage. Let the basketball people do the basketball, and take care of what he knew best—the business side, selling the team to corporations, sponsors and fans.

What helped Gilbert pull out of the swamp of doubt surrounding him was one of his basic "Isms," the first mentioned in the workbook given to new Quicken Employees: "It all starts with and ends with . . . Culture, Environment and Philosophy."

That sounds lofty and vague, but it does go to the heart of any organization: "Who are we? What are we about? What means the most to us?"

Those questions were in the back of his mind as he opened his search for a general manager.

"We talked to a ton of people," Gilbert said. "We talked to two guys from Denver [Jeff Weltman and Kiki Vandeweghe]. We talked to David Morway from Indiana. We talked to Randy Pfund from Miami. We talked to Greg Anthony from ESPN. I really liked him, but he didn't have much experience."

And he wanted to talk to Danny Ferry, who was an assistant general manager with the San Antonio Spurs. Gilbert had tremendous admiration for two franchises: Detroit and San Antonio. He believed they did more than just assemble talent, they knew how they wanted to play and they knew what kind of people they needed to make their approach work. They knew who they are and what they want to accomplish how what kind of people and organization was needed to make it happen.

"When we talked to these guys, I asked them what they'd do in their first week on the job, the first month and what they'd do six months into the job," said Gilbert. "We talked to 15-to-20 people, and most immediately began talking about getting a point guard, or filling some other position. They were very specific about what they wanted to do, and would name some players and coaches. With a few guys, it seemed I knew the salary cap better than they did—and that was a problem."

Most of these men were anxious for the job, which was very attractive. You had LeBron James, and that was critical. He would be the hub of your basketball solar system. Most teams were looking for their LeBron James, the sun that heats all the other planets. Then there was the fact that Paxson had put the Cavs in an enviable position of having about $28 million to spend on free agents.

Danny Ferry knew all that, but he wasn't sure that he wanted even be interviewed. It wasn't Cleveland. His wife was from Cleveland. Despite being the part of one of the worst trades in franchise history and a pro career that didn't come close to meeting his or anyone else's expectations, Ferry enjoyed most of his 10 years as a player with the Cavaliers. He liked the city, the people, the sports culture. One of his closest friends in pro sports is Indians General Manager Mark Shapiro. He loved to watch LeBron James play.

But there was Gilbert, and all the stories about him . . .

"I heard he was a problem," recalled Ferry.

Gilbert heard Ferry was one of the smartest young executives, and it was just a matter of time before he became a general manager. Ferry had been in the Spurs front office for only two years, but Gilbert didn't care about that.

"Experience can be overrated." he said. "You can be experienced, but are you any good?"

Gilbert believed that people with a lot of experience in their jobs can sometimes be too rigid, too unwillingly to see an old problem through a fresh set of eyes. There's a temptation for people who have done the same job for a long time to do the job the same way. It may be OK, but he wanted better than that. He needed better than OK. His man had to be much more than mediocre.

Initially, Ferry wasn't interested in interviewing for the Cavaliers' opening. The Cavs did receive permission to talk to Ferry from Spurs General Manager R.C. Buford and coach Gregg Popovich. Ferry talked to these two men, whom he considered his mentors. He decided to discuss the job with the Cavs, mostly to gain the experience of interviewing for a job as a general manager. In fact, Ferry could not recall the last time he interviewed for any job. He was a scholarship basketball player at Duke, one of the most sought after high school recruits in the county. Then he was a first round NBA draft choice, and received a 10-year contract from the Cavaliers. He played his final three seasons with the Spurs, who offered him a chance to work in the front office. He never had to sell himself to an employer.

Ferry even told his wife, "I don't want to leave San Antonio. This guy [Gilbert] sounds crazy. I don't think I'd get the job, anyway, but I do think it will be a good experience for me."

Ferry met with Gilbert and his main business partner, David Katzman, in Detroit. According to Gilbert, one of the first things Ferry said was, "I love San Antonio. It's a great town, a great organization. I love what I do. I don't know you guys. I don't know who you are or anything about you . . ."

Gilbert said he loved the straight approach, "Danny wasn't trying to sell. He was extremely loyal to who he was working for. One of the big differences between Danny and the others was when we asked him what would be the first things he'd do, he didn't talk about getting certain players. He didn't talk tactics. He was the only one who talked philosophy. He said we needed to create a team culture. He was talking our language."

When Ferry was pressed to talk about different players, he refused.

"He didn't want to answer because he believed that would give us some inclination of how the Spurs felt about certain coaches and players, and he didn't want to give that away," said Gilbert. "That appealed to me, his loyalty to the Spurs."

"I was thinking that I work for the Spurs, I'm probably not going to get hired here," said Ferry. "I'm going to be competing with them for free agents in the draft for players. They pushed me, but I was not going to back down. Instead, I talked to them about how character matters if you want to win. I talked about how to build an organization, how you put that process to work from scouting on up."

Then Ferry said, "I heard that you get involved too much. I don't want to come here if it's going to be like that. The basketball decisions have to be made by basketball people. We have to all be on the same page. There has to be trust. I'd keep you informed because it's a huge investment, but unless we're going over the salary cap and you'll have to pay the luxury tax, you need to leave the basketball to the basketball people. If it's not going to be that way, I don't know why I'd even think of coming here. Look, I don't know you guys. I'm interviewing you as much as you're interviewing me."

Gilbert told Ferry, "I don't want to make those decisions. I want to put people in place to do that."

When Ferry walked out of that first extended interview, he thought, "I don't think I'll get the job, but I feel very good about how I did."

Gilbert thought, "I like the guy a lot. But I'm not sure we can convince him to come here."

Ferry thought, "I really liked the guy. I'm surprised how much I like the guy. I like the 'Isms.' I think they are important, because they say who you are and what you believe. I love his passion. I think he's a good person."

Gilbert thought, "We need to talk to him more. This guy has great integrity and passion."

A call was made to Ferry, informing him the Cavs were interested in more discussions, but they planned to interview some other candidates.

Ferry thanked them and thought, "That's it. Fine with me. I can get back to work preparing for the draft with the Spurs."

This was happening when the Spurs were driving deep into the 2005 NBA playoffs, eventually knocking off Detroit in the Finals. Ferry continued to have talks with the Cavs during the playoffs. It was obvious the Cavs wanted to hire him.

But Gilbert said at one point, "We're not sure you really want the job."

Ferry said, "You're right, I'm not sure. I'm happy where I am."

Gilbert decided to wait. For this to work, Ferry had to make the next move. Ferry knew he was wanted. He knew the franchise, the city, the roster. He knew it was one of the best opportunities for a general manager in the last few years. Gilbert knew that Ferry was aware of all that. Now, both men had to find out how much Ferry wanted it.

Ferry was thinking, "This is a chance to try and do something special. I'm really getting to like Gilbert. I think he's learned a lot from what he went through. I believe him when he says he's looking for his own people to run it, and when he finds them, he'll let them do their jobs. What if this is the right thing for me, and I don't pursue it?"

A few days later, he called Gilbert and said, "I'm interested. But it has to be under the right circumstances."

They began to talk. Ferry was able to receive what he calls "clear language" that he was totally in charge of the basketball operation and he reported to only one man—Gilbert. He was surprised and pleased that Gilbert immediately agreed to it. Then they worked on the length of the contract, settling on five years. The money fell into place. Gilbert also was talking to coaching candidates, and was very impressed with Mike Brown. That was great news to Ferry. As they came close to a final deal, Ferry gave Gilbert a list of four men that he'd interview for the coaching vacancy. Brown was a prime candidate, because Brown was an assistant in San Antonio when Ferry played for the Spurs. The two men view the game the same way. Ferry was convinced he could work with Brown—and that Brown would be a positive influence on James and the other players, especially the younger ones. Brown was hired before Ferry, but that was only because the Spurs were involved in the playoffs and Ferry would not fully commit to the Cavs until San Antonio's season was over.

Suddenly, the Cavs had a new management team in place, and Danny Ferry was supposed to be a key to turning the franchise into a contender. But this time, he was greeted with more optimism than his first arrival. In his 10 years with the Cavaliers, Ferry made a lot of friends and earned respect from many fans because he handled a very difficult situation with grace and intelligence. There was a feeling when Gilbert hired Ferry, he turned the team over to a guy who knew and liked Cleveland. He wasn't Larry Brown, who seemed completely ill-suited for the job as general manager. None of the other candidates interviewed had any sizzle. Most were like Ferry, assistant general managers looking for a chance to run their own team. So why not Ferry? At least he's solid, sane and in many ways, a man who knew this franchise better than anyone as he played 10 years here.

This happened once before, the Cavaliers turning to Danny Ferry when trying to build a championship team. Cavs fans know it well, perhaps the worst deal in the history of the franchise—Ron Harper sent to the Los Angeles Clippers for the rights to Ferry. Basketball men such as Hall of Fame coach Lenny Wilkens and Cavs broadcaster Joe Tait believe that trade cost the Cavs a chance to upset the Bulls and win a title, because Harper was the kind of athletic, high-flying, scoring guard the Cavs lacked. He wasn't Jordan, but he was better than Craig Ehlo. No knock on Ehlo, who would have been a terrific sixth man on the Cavs teams of the early 1990s. But asking him to defend Jordan for 40 minutes in a playoff game was just too much. Harper may not have been able to match Jordan point-for-point, but he'd make Jordan run, sweat and even worry a bit. In his 228 games with the Cavaliers, Harper averaged 19.4 points, shot 47 percent and had nearly five assists and five rebounds. At 6-foot-6 and 200 pounds, he was the most athletic wing player in the history of the franchise until a kid named LeBron James showed up.

There's no need to go deep into the history of the trade. The Cavs front office was worried about some of Harper's friends. Coach Lenny Wilkens and General Manager Wayne Embry say that owner Gordon

Gund was behind the trade, demanding that Harper be moved. Gund says he was very concerned, but that neither Embry or Wilkens stood up to insist they keep Harper. The Cavs made a terrible deal, sending not just Harper but TWO future first round picks to the Clippers for journeyman guard Reggie Williams and the rights to Ferry, who was playing in Italy because he had no interest in being a Los Angeles Clipper. They traded Harper only seven games into the 1989–90 season, and Ferry would play that entire year in Rome. It became a public relations disaster, starting with a trade night press release quoting Embry saying, "Boston had to wait a year for Larry Bird and San Antonio waited two years for David Robinson. We aren't putting Danny in Bird's class, but we think he'll be worth the wait."

Then the Cavs gave Ferry a staggering 10-year, $33 million contract. Before he ever stepped on an NBA court, Ferry became the Cavs' highest paid player on a very good team featuring the likes of Mark Price, Brad Daugherty and Larry Nance. Ferry struggled with the Cavs, especially early in his career when he seldom started and often was on the end of the bench. Many fans saw him as yet another Cleveland sports heartbreak—The Deal That Went Wrong.

"Before I took the job, I thought about the trade and how people reacted," said Ferry. "But I liked my time in Cleveland. I think people accepted me in those 10 years. And this was a great chance to build a winner."

Ferry rarely talks about his playing career, but he opened his heart when talking for this book.

"The first year that I came here, I had a microfracture in my knee," he said. "I played with it. But I wasn't the same player."

The 6-foot-10, 230-pound Ferry joined a team that didn't need a power forward, which was probably his best position. The 1990–91 Cavaliers had Larry Nance and John Williams at that position. The hope was Ferry could play small forward, but his knee restricted his mobility and he suffered on defense against smaller, quicker players. He also struggled to get off his shots against the better athletes. Ferry refused to make an issue of the knee. He knew great things were expected, big money was paid, and no one wanted to hear excuses— even if they were valid.

"I played with it for a few years, then I had knee surgery on one leg—it was torn cartilage," he said. "I told them to look at the other knee because it hurt, and they were like—*wow*—this knee is worse than the first one. It was the microfracture."

Ferry averaged 8.6 points and shot 43 percent as a rookie for an injury-ravaged team that was 33-49. Late in that season Ferry told the *Akron Beacon Journal*, "I never expected to be this bad." Ferry had been the NCAA college basketball Player of the Year in 1989. He averaged 22 points for Duke, and some did compare him to Larry Bird because of his passing and shooting skills. He was a great college player.

"Looking back, I can see that I felt the pressure, but I didn't want to admit it," Ferry said. "I internalized it. I put so much pressure on myself. It got to the point where I was totally lost."

After failing to make it as a small forward during his rookie season, the Cavs suggested he try to play center. He needed to get bigger and stronger, so he went from 228 pounds to 258 pounds. Not a good idea. Already having problems with quickness, the extra weight made him slower. It also didn't help his knee troubles, which he was still trying to play through rather than face surgery.

"At no point in my career could I jump that high," Ferry said. "But this took away any athletic ability I had in my left leg. I just kept taking anti-inflammatories and trying to play through it."

In his third season, Ferry played 20 minutes a game off the bench, averaging 7.5 points, shooting 47 percent and helping as a role player for a team that was 53-29. He said Coach Lenny Wilkens "probably didn't want me here at first, but he started to grow in appreciation for what I could do in that third season. I was feeling really good about things, and he left."

In the summer of 1993, Wilkens and the Cavs had a mutual parting at the request of the coach. Mike Fratello was hired, and Ferry thought he had a fresh start. It became the worst season of his pro career as he rarely played. Fratello thought Ferry was a liability on defense. But he was four years into that 10-year deal, "The contract made me untradeable. I couldn't go anywhere else. And candidly, I wasn't going to walk away from all that money. Sometimes, I didn't feel good about getting all this money, and not playing and not producing. I had times when I thought, 'I played so well at Duke, and I can't even get off the bench in the NBA?' The summer after Fratello's first year, I felt helpless and hopeless."

Duke coach Mike Krzyzewski began to tell Ferry to "quit looking over your shoulder [at the coach] when you make a bad play." He told Ferry that he was "too self critical." He suggested Ferry see a sports psychologist, which a desperate Ferry agreed to do.

"I got a lot out of that," said Ferry. "I did learn a lot about myself. I had lost all my joy in playing the game. I learned I was always looking for approval from others. I began to read some psychology books, and really study. I read a book called *Thinking Body, Dancing Mind* by Jerry Lynch. I mean, I read it about 30 times. Then I read *The Inner Game Of Tennis* about 20 times. I read a lot, and I became a sponge."

Ferry had knee surgery. He dropped a lot of weight, down to about 220. He worked on his quickness. He turned himself into an adequate small forward on defense with a deadly 3-point shot. From 1994–97, he played in every game, averaging about 11 points and shooting nearly 40 percent from 3-point range. A great player? No. But he was effective.

"I loved it," he said. "My joy for basketball came back. I enjoyed those years in Cleveland. I met my wife there and we got married in 1995. When my contract came up after the 10 years, I signed with the Spurs—and came off the bench for three years with them. That was the most fun I had in the NBA, because the team was so good, the organization strong. I was playing for the minimum salary. It was a relief. The people like Pop [Gregg Popovich] made it so special, I felt like I was back at Duke. I was on a championship team. I would have played forever there if I could. I was really proud to be a part of Duke, and the same in San Antonio. I felt like I was part of something special."

So what does Ferry's playing career have to do with him as the Cavaliers general manager?

His failures and frustrations give him greater insight into struggling players. To become average, he had to not only work physically and change his body—he had to grow psychologically. He had to study the game, and study how the mind works. He took the criticism during his early years in Cleveland and played through the pain of his knees.

Joe Tait often says Ferry was perhaps his favorite Cavalier player because he dealt with so many setbacks, and because he handled the attacks in the media without lashing back.

"For all those years, it was Danny was a stiff, he's no good, he's the guy we got for Harper, blah, blah, blah," said Tait. "He worked through it. We were not that close when he played. We talked, but I have become closer to him now that he's the general manager. I just admired him for his work ethic and his character. And I never heard Danny speak about his career, or complain about the criticism—not once."

Wayne Embry remembers seeing Ferry come to the arena late at night—after a morning practice—to work on his jumper. His wife, Tiffany, would be there to rebound for him. Embry talks about how Ferry had a 10-year contract. He could have just "sat on the money." He could have sulked and forced the Cavs to cut him, to pay him off. Instead, he kept searching for a way to help the team.

"In San Antonio, I discovered a role player is valued more on a good team because they give him more value," said Ferry. "The coaches valued me. They loved the fact that I wasn't a great athlete but it didn't matter. I tried. I could do some things to help a team. In San Antonio, I found myself a bit."

All these experiences put him on the fast track to becoming an NBA general manager, much more than growing up the son of Bob Ferry, a veteran NBA general manager in Washington. More than his success at Duke. Obviously, a father makes a major impact. So does a college program such as Duke. But most people learn more from pain and heartache than they do from victory and praise. He understands some of the pressure on James because he felt it himself when had such a great career at Duke and came into the NBA with a huge contract and outrageous expectations. But he also is more sympathetic to bench players than some general managers, because he knows what it means to be unsure of when you'll play—and how that can impact your confidence. He also knows the mindset needed not just to be a star, but to be a reserve on a winning team.

"Danny knew our locker room better than anyone," said Spurs General Manager R.C. Buford. "He could talk to the starters, and he could talk to the guys at the end of the bench. He understood how a team is put together. It wasn't long before we were talking to him about free agents we were thinking of signing."

All of this while Ferry was still playing for the Spurs.

"That's why I approached him about working in the front office," said Gregg Popovich. "For some former players, they are used to just going to practice for a couple of hours in the morning, then going home. That's just the start of the day for the coaches and the front office. I'm not surprised the Cavaliers hired Danny. He was too hard working, too smart, too good for someone not to grab him."

Gilbert called Gund when he was considering Ferry for the job. Gund immediately gave Ferry a strong endorsement. He had been telling friends for years that he thought Ferry and Steve Kerr were the two former Cavalier players who'd make excellent executives. Kerr was hired as the Phoenix Suns general manager in the summer of 2007.

"Danny is smart with high integrity and he was the kind of player who always wanted to fit in and encourage others," said Gund. "I look back at his career and I think the year in Italy didn't help him. Then he should have allowed himself time to heal the first year, but he wanted to play because of all the expectations. He had the 10-year contract, he could have laid down and took the money. He never did. He's a worker. I respect that."

Embry is proud of Ferry now running the franchise that he helped put on a winning course in the middle 1980s. He's confident Ferry will find the right guys to play with LeBron James.

"I just gave Danny one bit of advice," said Embry. "Never give anyone a 10-year contract."

It seemed Gilbert did this backwards, hiring Mike Brown three weeks before Ferry. You never hire a coach before you hire a general manager. It's hard enough for a general manager and coach to get along when the coach was hired by the general manager. The last thing you want is a shotgun basketball marriage, because the general manager has an immediate excuse when the team falters—hey, it's the coach. I didn't even hire the guy, so don't blame me.

But Brown and Ferry were part of Gilbert's dream package.

"Because Danny was in the playoffs with the Spurs, he didn't want to announce that he was coming here—even though we had permission to talk to Danny from the Spurs and they gave him their blessing," said Gilbert. "Mike Brown was close to Danny, and we knew Danny liked him. Mike was an assistant with Indiana, and they were knocked out of the playoffs early. Several teams were looking at Mike, and we didn't want to lose him."

When Brown was hired, he was 35, had never played in the NBA or been a head coach at any level. He was a guy who crawled up the NBA ladder the hard way, making stops at every rung as he began as an intern and video coordinator in Denver, an assistant under Gregg Popovich in San Antonio, then the top assistant coach for Rick Carlisle with Indiana.

"In a 45-minute interview, Mike Brown impressed me more than anyone I've interviewed in my life," said Gilbert. "He was a guy with every tool in the toolbox. He had a philosophy, a culture and real character. Calling around, we couldn't find anyone to say a bad word about the guy. He's worked his tail off. We sensed he'd be a great guy for LeBron. He was not too young or too old. He could communicate well and clearly. He knew how to listen. I wasn't worried about his lack of experience as a head coach, because the experienced head coaches we talked to didn't overly impress us."

The biggest name was Flip Saunders, who spent 10 years with Minnesota. While Gilbert won't comment on it, supposedly the owner was concerned about Saunders' lack of playoff success. He had an excellent winning percentage of .560 in the regular season, but he survived the first round of the playoffs just once. Gilbert supposedly wasn't impressed by Saunders' answers about his playoff struggles, and thought the veteran coach was too defensive rather than addressing the issue head on. Had Jim Paxson and Mark Warkentein remained, Saunders would have been the next head coach since Paul Silas had been fired. They believed a reliable veteran coach was critical to advancing James' career.

Gilbert first looked at what he considered the most successful organizations in the modern NBA. They were not necessarily those that won the most titles. But they were consistent contenders with a clear approach to how they wanted to play.

"I looked at Detroit and at San Antonio," said Gilbert. "Just watching the playoffs, you could see teams winning with defense. Those were defensive teams. You see Phoenix every year *not* make the Finals, and teams that stressed defense did. So that told me that we wanted a defensive coach."

Interestingly, Saunders was rejected by the Cavs, but quickly re-cruited by Detroit when things shattered with Larry Brown. Yes, Larry Brown loomed somewhere in the shadows of the Cavaliers situation, but it seemed Gilbert figured out that the veteran coach had too many physical problems and emotional ups and downs to take on rebuild-ing the Cavaliers. Gilbert did talk to Eric Musselman, and liked the former Golden State coach very much for his preparation.

But he had the combination of Ferry and Brown in mind, bringing some of that San Antonio savvy north to Cleveland.

"No matter who I talked to, they raved about Mike Brown," said Gilbert. "Donnie Walsh [Indiana Pacers president] raved about him. [Pacers coach] Rick Carlisle raved about him. Bernie Bickerstaff [coach and GM of the Charlotte Bobcats] raved about him. Popovich raved about him and Danny Ferry. They also said he was a defensive-oriented coach, and that was what we wanted. In Indiana, Mike was the associate head coach. Carlisle turned the defense over to him and let Mike put in his own defense, and Rick let Mike run it as he saw fit. We talked to so many players who loved Mike. It also was very important that Danny wanted Mike, because we were trying to close the deal with Danny."

Popovich said Brown was the least experienced of his assistants when hired by San Antonio in 2000, "but within two weeks, I had him giving scouting reports to our team. He has great communication skills. Players have a real B.S. antenna, and they immediately saw Mike as a genuine guy . . . We lost Mike because Indiana doubled his salary and gave him a new title [associate head coach]. Those guys [Ferry and Brown] were prepared to take over [in Cleveland]."

Consider that Gilbert became wealthy based on his ability to sell. He not only operated in the realm of ideas, but in the cold, hard, no-excuse world of execution. One of his "Isms" reads: "Innovation is rewarded. Execution is worshipped. A great idea is just a first step. The real magic is bringing that ideas to life with great execution."

What does that have to do with hiring Mike Brown?

Everything.

When Brown has an idea, he states it clearly, and doesn't back down from it. He believes teams win with defense and rebounding. Most coaches say that, not all demand it of their players. They give mixed messages. Yes, we want to defend, but we also want to out-score the other guy. Their discussion of defense turns murky, vague and isn't backed by actions. They tolerate poor defense. Brown not only talked defense, but had a few very understandable ways that he planned to implement it.

In addition to his "Isms," Gilbert has a list of 21 things that he's learned from life and business. One of them reads: "Light yourself on fire and many people will join your mission."

After listening to Brown for 45 minutes, Gilbert was ready to take the court and try and draw a charging foul. Gilbert believed if Brown could sell a salesman such as himself, he could sell the current players and possible free agents on his vision for the Cavaliers.

But Gilbert also was gambling on Ferry not changing his mind. Three weeks before Ferry joined the team, he was still with the Spurs, still had not signed with the Cavs, still having serious discussions with his wife about moving—they both love San Antonio, as do their children. It could have fallen apart, and Gilbert would have had a coach—but no general manager.

"We really didn't have a No. 2 candidate at that point," admitted Gilbert. "Mark Warkentein was still with us, and he could have run the draft. We only had a second-round pick. But the field was thin. Danny was our guy."

Even putting Brown and Ferry together was a risk. Neither had experience in the jobs for which they were being hired. When the Cavs last went that route with Jim Paxson and Randy Wittman, the results were not good. Both men had periods of being overwhelmed and having to not only learn some things the hard way, but learn them for the first time. Gilbert was trusting that a rookie general manager and a rookie coach could turn the franchise around within a year to the point where LeBron James would feel confident enough to sign a contract extension.

That meant Ferry had to upgrade the roster, and do it quick. It meant Brown had to take the new players, blend them with the old, and then build a team that truly had a defensive mindset. It meant that Gilbert had to be right . . . right that this was the right time and the right place for these two men—both under 40—to make the Cavaliers attractive to James and a contender in the very near future.

CHAPTER 17

"A PENNY SAVED IS JUST A PENNY"

Building around LeBron

Danny Ferry was stunned during one of his first meetings with his new boss after taking the job in the summer of 2005 when Dan Gilbert asked, "If we take money out of the equation, what is the best way to do this?"

Gilbert was talking about changes to Quicken Loans Arena and the dressing room. Ferry realized that Gilbert was very serious about his "Isms," the proverbs that govern Gilbert's approach to business. One of them reads: "Numbers and money follow, they don't lead. Don't chase money. Chase the skills that will make you great at what you are doing or what you are building."

Gilbert asked Ferry what it would take to make the Cavaliers into a championship team, beyond such obvious answers as talented players and coaches.

What would appeal to stars such as James? What could be done to make them believe in the organization? What would be necessary to create an atmosphere so that they'd want to stay in Cleveland?

Ferry slowly began talking about state-of-the-art dressing rooms with plush carpeting, DVD players and individual TV sets in each locker, so a player could study personal game videos. He talked about building a practice facility away from downtown Cleveland. He waited for Gilbert to bring up the cost, but the owner was more interested in the ideas—and the benefits that would come from them. He already was in the mindset of having an elite dressing room to attract players, based on what owner Mark Cuban had done with the Dallas Mavericks. Ferry stressed what Gilbert already knew: It was crucial to keep LeBron James. Cleveland is not No. 1 on the list of favorite places for most players, so everything has to be first class.

No problem, insisted Gilbert, thinking of another of his "Isms": "A penny saved is just a penny."

It didn't take long before the old lockers were removed. New, larger, deeper wooden ones were installed. In addition to the TV sets, Xbox consoles and stereo systems were added to each locker. The coaches' offices were remodeled. A large family lounge was built with play areas for the children of players and coaches. Giant TVs and lots of food were available in an upscale atmosphere.

"We hired a full-time chef to be there so our players can get breakfast, lunch and dinner—any time they want to eat, they can eat at the arena," said Coach Mike Brown. "I'd rather have them eating our food because it will be healthier for them than what some of the guys would buy for themselves. On the road, we set up team meals at the hotel. I think it also gives the guys a good place to hang out and talk."

Better than McDonalds, the food court at the mall or a bar.

Gilbert loved the idea. It's exactly the kind of thing he does for his employees at Quicken Loans.

Gilbert also put nearly $16 million into the arena, starting with new seats, new scoreboards, a new playing floor and upgraded concourses. He knew the improvements could not inspire many more ticket sales. James already was helping to sell out most home games. Gilbert also invested about $25 million to build a new practice facility in Independence.

"This guy spares no expense," Cavs veteran radio broadcaster Joe Tait said.

When Gordon Gund owned the team, he kept the arena in good condition, but there weren't any significant additions. The Cavaliers also spent time making sure they didn't have to pay rent under their deal with Gateway Corporation, charging any improvement they made against payments due on the lease. For several years, they paid no rent. In the last few years of Gund's ownership, there was a sense he was looking for someone with more energy to buy the team—and that became Gilbert in the spring of 2005.

"Let's just say we have a lot more resources now to work with," said Tad Carper, the Cavaliers' vice president of communications. "If you have a good idea, there is money to get it done."

Such as changing the color scheme of the arena and uniforms to maroon, gold and white.

"There was nothing wrong with the old royal-blue seats," said Gilbert. "I just thought they looked like garbage on TV. You can have only 10 percent of them open, and it seemed like half the arena was empty. So we spent $3 million on the maroon seats to just brighten up the arena."

He did the same with the floor, the scoreboards and the high-quality sound system. He brought in bands to entertain fans and baskets for them to shoot at in the parking lot before some games. There were face painters for young fans.

"Dan just wanted to liven up the atmosphere," said Pat McInnis, Quicken Loans president. "He wasn't worried about how it would pay off, but he knew it would."

Gilbert believes it did when the Cavs signed a lucrative 10-year TV deal with Fox Sports. He said it's "the third-best local deal in the NBA. I know having No. 23 [James] had a lot to do with it, but they also said they sense my commitment to the team by what we did at the arena—and that was why they went out 10 years on the contract."

During games, Gilbert watches the game presentation just as Ferry studies the game itself. He doesn't want to miss anything. He's constantly asking himself what can be done better. The Cavs' Carper said he never has seen anyone "so aware of his surroundings" as Gilbert. He talked about Gilbert's "360 rule." That means no matter where you sit or stand in or around the arena, you should be able to see a Cavs logo and a Quicken Loans logo if you turn in a circle.

"On the walls, on the floor, in the elevators, everywhere," said Carper. "He changed the Quicken logo on the floor so it will always be right side up when the cameras catch it."

Gilbert wants the identity of the Cavs and Quicken Loans to mesh. He changed the name of the arena from Gund Arena to Quicken Loans Arena. The arena walls have life-size pictures of LeBron James and other athletes stuck to them—from a company called Fathead, which he also owns. From a business sense, buying the Cavaliers for $375 million gave notice that Gilbert really is a major player in the business world. As Quicken Loans Vice President Elizabeth Jones said: "Because we're not a public company [traded on the stock markets], there has always been some discussion of how we are doing. Buying the Cavs was another sign that we're doing well."

Gilbert wants to keep it that way, and to keep fans happy.

"He didn't like the carpet on the ends of the floor because it didn't match the seat colors," said Carper. "So he changed it. That doesn't sell any tickets, but Dan keeps telling us, 'Just do what is right.'"

In his presentation to new Quicken Loans employees, Gilbert mentioned going to last season's All-Star Game at the "TA Center" in Houston. He showed a slide of a burned-out sign from the Toyota Center, where only the letters T and A were lighted. "Every sign burns out," he said. "Ours does. The question is what to do about it. I was there for three days. Three days when everyone is watching the All-Star Game. They never fixed it. That made me wonder if anyone noticed. Or did they notice—and even worse—not care?"

Gilbert mentioned how a few letters on his Quicken Loans building burned out. They immediately shut down the sign, spent a day fixing the problem, then turned the sign back on when all the letters were lighted.

Fixing the team was not quite as easy.

Danny Ferry met LeBron James for the first time at the press conference where he was named general manager.

"Hi, I'm looking forward to working with you," said James.

Ferry noticed his young star was quiet, business-like. He appreciated the gesture, showing up for the press conference. That was a sign of respect, something players don't always show to management. Clearly, James wanted to begin the relationship the right way. Ferry talked briefly with James, and they departed. He knew that James wanted Zydrunas Ilgauskas back. He had said so several times in the final months of the season. Ferry was delighted, because he also was a big fan of the team's center. One of the first things Ferry did after attending the press conference was to call his old friend, Ilgauskas. The veteran Cavs center was a free agent, and Ilgauskas had heard that the new owners were not enamored with him.

"Continuity is an important part of a franchise," said Ferry. "I don't think they [ownership] really knew Z. They'd only seen Ben Wallace [from Detroit]. The big thing to me was Mike [Brown] believed he could get Z to be an effective defensive player in his system. Z is

7-foot-3 and that kind of length is important in being able to defend the basket. Mike came from San Antonio where they had David Robinson and Tim Duncan—two very long guys who can block shots. Z is not a physical player like Ben Wallace, but he can block shots."

This was one of Gilbert's first tests.

His basketball people wanted Ilgauskas, so he gave the OK to sign Ilgauskas. As Ferry and Brown explained to the owner, you have to consider the options. You can't go get Tim Duncan, he's under contract with San Antonio. David Robinson is retired. Shaquille O'Neal is with Miami. Ilgauskas was, by far, the best center available. He also had the character that would be a part of the culture they wanted to create. He liked Cleveland and had married a Cleveland girl. He loved playing with LeBron James, and James appreciated Ilgauskas. He didn't care about being the center of attention. The center on a championship team was more important. In the summer of 2005, Ilgauskas had turned 30. He had been with the Cavaliers since 1997, playing for six different coaches. Mike Brown would be his seventh in seven years. He just wanted a sense of stability, a reason to believe the franchise was headed in the proper direction. Hiring Ferry had been a signal of that, because they had played together and were good friends with the Cavs. He thought Ferry could be trusted.

Signing Ilgauskas was complex. He had made $14.6 million in the 2004–05 season and the Cavs were asking him to take a significant pay cut, nearly half his salary. Then there were his feet, which had endured five operations. They had been healthy for four years, but there were insurance issues with the contract. There is an NBA rule requiring teams to get insurance on their five highest-paid players. They can cover up to 80 percent of the value. But with Ilgauskas' history, the team would have to assume most of the risk. Those things could be worked out with negotiations, but it was just as important to sell Ilgauskas on the new franchise setup. He and Ferry were very close from their playing days in Cleveland, when the Cavs came to San Antonio the two would usually have dinner together. As for the new owner and the new coach, Ilgauskas wasn't so sure. Like most people close to the Cavs, Ilgauskas heard that Gilbert—or at least those close to him—thought he was a liability in the middle. Too slow, didn't score enough, didn't block enough shots or play physical defense. Ferry re-

alized Ilgauskas needed to feel wanted. Spending time around basketball will tell you that big men are often very sensitive. Their size makes
them feel very out-of-place everywhere except on the court. People
sometimes say some very stupid and insulting things, "Hey, big guy,
how's the weather up there?" Because they are so much bigger than
most people, they aren't supposed to respond physically. They just
take it. As children, they are taught to play carefully. "You don't want
to hurt the other boys and girls, you are so much bigger and stronger."

Ilgauskas averaged 16.9 points and 8.6 rebounds in 2004–05, and
certainly believed he did his part to help the team. In the previous
three seasons, he had missed a grand total of five games. He proved he
was healthy. Ferry agreed on all points, and began recruiting Ilgauskas
as if he were a prized free agent who had never played in Cleveland.
It was a wise strategy. When talks became intense, Ferry hatched an
idea he thought might put a bow on things. Ilgauskas and his wife were
planning on leaving for a trip to China and he knew they were flying
to Los Angeles before catching a connecting flight across the Pacific.
Ferry was in Cleveland, but the two people he needed to sell Ilgauskas
on, Brown and Gilbert, were in Las Vegas for the Cavs summer league.

He called Gilbert and said, "How about you and coach meeting Z
and his wife at the airport," he said.

"What airport?" asked Gilbert.

"Los Angeles," said Ferry.

Ferry's plan was for the coach and owner to show up in Los Angeles
and surprise Ilgauskas with a pitch. Brown hopped on Gilbert's private
jet in Vegas for the 50-minute flight to Los Angeles International
Airport. When the two arrived, they unexpectedly bumped into Seattle
Supersonics owner Howard Schultz as he was getting off his private
jet. The Sonics had salary-cap space, too, and Gilbert thought the plan
to court Ilgauskas may not have been an original one. Maybe Seattle
was after the big man. Gilbert's juices were bubbling. Schultz was a
hot executive, just like himself. In catching a car to take them to the
main terminal, Gilbert ordered his driver to follow Schultz, the CEO
of Starbucks. But Schultz's limo got on the highway. He was not after
Ilgauskas. Gilbert had his driver now take them back to the airport.
Gilbert and Brown, having bought first-class tickets they never in-
tended to use just so they could get past security, headed to meet the

7-foot-3 Lithuanian. That's right, they bought *first class* tickets just to get through security. Talk about not counting pennies—or hundreds. But they were two guys with no luggage and two one-way first class tickets, and this made the security people very nervous in the post-9/11 world. Brown was allowed to pass through, but Gilbert was pulled out of line and nearly stripped-searched. Leaving Gilbert with the authorities, Brown jogged down the terminal concourse looking for his center. Too late, they had gone to a different terminal for a different flight. Brown returned to security, where Gilbert had finally been cleared. Bad news, the coach said, they are not here. He explained the new destination as they jumped in a Hertz van to take them to another terminal. This time, they made it through security.

As they walked down the concourse, Brown saw a store, ducked in and bought a balloon reading I LOVE YOU, along with some flowers.

"Do you think that's a good idea?" asked Gilbert.

"It's for Z's wife." said Brown.

"Oh," said Gilbert.

They found Ilgauskas and his wife. She gushed about the flowers and balloon. They had lunch. They talked. The couple boarded a flight to Asia for their summer vacation.

"Thirty minutes after the flight left, my phone rang," said Ferry. "It was Z's agent. He said Mike and Dan had done a very smart thing and Z wanted to make a deal. We got it done that night."

The contract was $53 million for five years, and it was settled by late July. But it wasn't officially announced until the middle of September so the Cavs would have some ability to make small adjustments to help their cap and sign others players. Ilgauskas agreed to that. Not every player would. But Ilgauskas sincerely believed in Ferry, and was touched by what Brown and Gilbert had done. He never wanted to leave Cleveland, and the Cavs gave him reason to stay. Had he gone on the open market, he probably would have received an even larger contract.

Ferry had to move fast.

The Cavs had to add players, quick, because the free agent market was shrinking by the day. The clock was ticking. They had to add talent *now*, to *win* now. Armed with the discipline of previous general manager Jim Paxson and some rules in the brand new NBA Collective Bargaining Agreement, the Cavs found themselves with $28 million in salary cap space. Since the cap came in the early 1980s, no team ever had that much money to spend. It was also a challenge because some new cap rules left eight teams with significant salary-cap space, which was also record setting. But Cleveland had not been to the playoffs in seven years, had an unattractive income tax structure compared to other states, and the team was on its sixth coach in six years. Players also like warm weather cities: Phoenix, Miami, the Lakers, the Texas teams. Cleveland was not exactly high on the vacation list for most of these guys. Ferry was going to have to bring lots of cash to the table to land a major free agent.

As Ferry said, "We have an obligation to help LeBron, to put pieces around him to develop his game and the team. We have to build around him, and build the right way. That summer, we had to make a statement not just to LeBron, but to our other players, our fans, our organization that we were going to be aggressive and we were out to win. We could not afford to miss the playoffs again.'"

After missing the playoffs in the first two seasons, they had to get in the post-season . . . *now!* It was part of an effort to convince James to sign an extension of his contract the next summer. The Cavs were going to have to overpay for talent—something Northeast Ohio fans had been begging their teams to do for years.

They targeted four players they wanted, all shooting guards. All in position to get large contracts. Shooting guard was a position of need for the Cavs. During the 2004–05 season they started Ira Newble there most nights. Newble is a defensive reserve specialist. The starting backcourt for 2004–05 of Eric Snow and Newble averaged 9.9 points, the lowest in the league. They needed a shooting guard who could put the ball in the hoop. One of Ferry's goal was to surround James with some outside shooters. It also was why he was so intent on retaining Ilgauskas. A strong case could be made that the center was the best medium range shooter on the team. Shooting would open up the middle for James to drive and also help him against double-teamed defenses, as he could throw the ball to an open man who, ideally, makes the open jump shot.

On the market were Ray Allen, Joe Johnson, Larry Hughes and Michael Redd. The two biggest names were Redd and Allen, but they were also the two longest shots. The cap rules favor teams signing their own free agents, allowing them to sign for an extra year and to get bigger annual raises. In the case of Allen and Redd, both of whom signed max contracts to stay at home in Seattle and Milwaukee respectively, that meant an extra $20 million guaranteed. The Cavs courted both and even hosted Redd in Cleveland on a visit, but the difference was too much to ignore. An Ohio State product, Redd was intrigued by the Cavs. But not to the point where he'd give up the extra $20 million that the Bucks could pay.

For the Cavs, the good news was these cap rules would help them later keep James—no team can offer more money or more years than a player's original franchise. But now, it hurt their attempts to lure Allen and Redd. The Cavs were also wary about Johnson; he was a restricted free agent so the Phoenix Suns could match any deal.

"The Suns wanted a draft pick," said Ferry. "Because of some previous deals, we didn't have any to trade."

Phoenix traded Johnson to the Atlanta Hawks, but it cost a quality player in Boris Diaw and two first round draft picks. So Ferry went after a guy he thought he could get, Hughes.

Sometimes, getting The Guy means getting the best guy available, maybe not your first choice. But he is better than what you have, and you have to get someone—now. Especially if you want to keep the player who truly is The Guy.

Hughes wasn't a great shooter, like Allen and Redd. The Cavs liked Hughes because he thrived in a system with the Washington Wizards' other stars, Gilbert Arenas and Antawn Jamison. In Cleveland, he'd have to play with James, and he seemed to have the temperament that didn't demand that he be the star. The last thing they wanted was another Ricky Davis. Hughes also was known for being a good defender, named to the All-Defensive Team in 2005. He was 25 years old and coming off a career season in which he led the led the NBA in steals and averaged 22 points, 6.3 rebounds and 4.7 assists per game. Great numbers. A concern was his injury history. In the previous three seasons, he missed an average of 19 games with various injuries. Mike Brown was a defensive coach, and the lanky 6-foot-5 Hughes should fit into his system. Brown also liked the fact that Hughes had solid ballhandling skills, good enough to play some point guard.

But best of all, he was an unrestricted free agent, meaning he could sign with the Cavs. Washington could not match any offer. He wanted to return to Washington, but was upset when the Wizards offered him a six-year deal that averaged $9 million per season. Unlike the case with Redd and Allen, Hughes' team was not going to offer a maximum contract. The Cavs could out-bid the Wizards, and get their guy. It wasn't like the Cavs had a choice between Oscar Robertson or Jerry West in their primes and Larry Hughes—but Hughes was, by far, the best guard available. Ferry heard Washington's offer, and countered with a five-year deal that started at $10.3 million. It could be worth up to $70 million with incentives. That $10.3 number didn't come from thin air. The Cavs had done their research and learned Hughes had been telling people he wanted at least the same amount team-mate Arenas made. Arenas' salary for the upcoming season was $10.2 million. The Wizards attempted to match the Cavs offer, but Hughes had made up his mind to leave. It was the biggest and richest outside free agent deal in Cavs team history.

Did they overpay?

Of course they did.

Just as they overpaid to bring in role players Donyell Marshall and Damon Jones, two veterans who had reputations as outside shooters.

But the point was to add players who could help . . . *now*.

Win . . . *now*.

There was a sense of mission and urgency the franchise had not experienced in years. Yes, those contracts were big. Yes, they would be an obstacle on the cap in a few years, especially in the cases of Jones and Marshall who signed for four years. But both players had been offered three years by other teams, and the Cavs needed help . . . *now*.

But adding these pieces helped the Cavaliers keep their guy, and set up a run for the NBA title in 2007.

CHAPTER 18

REASONS TO STICK AROUND

_____

The clock starts ticking

When it came to LeBron James, the Cavaliers were on the clock in the fall of 2005.

Dan Gilbert agreed to buy the Cavaliers early in the 2004–05 season, but the deal wasn't approved by the league until March 2005. In the four months before he took over, Gilbert and his partners at his venture capital firm spent hours poring over the Cavs books, reading NBA rules and doing background checks by having dozens of conversations with people around the team and the league. That's how Gilbert did things. When he took on any venture, he dug deep. Details were everything, the "inches" that Gilbert often talks about as being the difference between success and failure. As he wrote in his Quicken Loans manual: "The inches we need are everywhere around us. Opportunities for us to make a difference are everywhere, and they usually are found in the little things . . . it's 1,001 of these little things that add up to who we are."

Gilbert had to convince James and the player's advisors that he was the owner who could make the Cavaliers a contender and the place where James would want to stay. That took work. That took research. That took a team effort from ownership.

His business partner and fellow owner, David Katzman, spearheaded this effort. As Katzman once said, "Dan finds the bones, I dig them up." Sounds a little creepy, but another of Gilbert's mottos has to do with "going deep" to solve problems. Well, they took out the shovels and flashlights, searching to find all they could about James and what mattered most to the kid from Akron.

When James was drafted in 2003, he signed a standard rookie contract slotting him to earn a little more than $12 million over three years. Two months into his first season, the Cavs picked up the option for his fourth year, which was for about $6 million. Under NBA rules, teams can extend their draft picks contracts following their third season. So while he was signed up for four years, they could talk extension after the third season. That made the summer of 2006 a deadline of sorts for the Cavs. They certainly would present James with a maximum contract offer, the most they could pay under salary cap rules—and it also would be more than any other team could offer.

With James earning most of his money from endorsements, the maximum contract might not have been enough. He wanted to be a place where he could win and be comfortable in doing so. That created a sense of urgency within the new organization, and they embraced it. Another of Gilbert's "Isms" reads: "Responding with a sense of urgency is the ante to play." Gilbert believed passion, energy and urgency is what made Quicken Loans a success, and he was determined to use the same approach to retain James.

In the spring and early summer of 2005, the Cavs had the look of a team in disarray as there was no coach and no general manager following their late season collapse that cost them a playoff berth. They only had a handful of players under contract and didn't have any draft picks. Yes, new GM Danny Ferry had $28 million of salary cap room to use for new players. But James just endured two years of two coaches, two owners, a changing roster and frustrating finishes to each season. He had to be asking himself, "Do the new guys know what they are doing?"

Gilbert and his management team had to prove themselves, and do it quickly. That's why they overpaid for free agents such as Larry Hughes, Donyell Marshall and Damon Jones. The future was now, and the future is James. If they didn't begin to win now—the 2005–06 season—they could lose James. They had to sell him on the future by creating success in the present.

Gilbert had a three-part plan to keep James.

First, he wanted to surround his young star with more talent, which became feasible with the $28 million in salary-cap room he inherited that first summer. Gilbert ended up committing to contracts for new players worth more than $150 million.

Second, he wanted to upgrade the creature comforts for the players. That involved an investment of about $40 million. There were physical improvements, like the palatial new practice facility south of the city to be ready by the fall of 2007, and a renovated locker room at the arena set for the fall of 2006. He provided meals after every practice, every shoot-around and every game. The Cavs added a team of masseurs who even traveled with them on the road so players could be cared for daily. He upgraded the team jet, leasing a bigger model that had more range so the team wouldn't have to stop and refuel when going to the West Coast. Those were all high-profile moves. It fit into Gilbert's philosophy of "Money doesn't lead, it follows." Or the old saying, "You gotta spend some to make more." By making these investments, it was not only a signal to James—but all the players—that Gilbert planned to have a first class franchise.

The third part of the plan wasn't seen by the fans or media.

Gilbert's research revealed that James was very close with his friends, whom he trusted deeply. The bond was so tight that James was leaning towards firing his successful first agent, Aaron Goodwin, and turning his management and marketing over to his friends— especially confidant Maverick Carter, who got a job with Nike as a part of James' shoe deal. Carter had been preparing to become a marketing agent himself. While James always insisted that he was the one who made all the decisions, he was fond of saying his friends' opinions and feelings influenced him. Rather than only reaching out to Goodwin and James' mother Gloria, Gilbert knew establishing a foundation with James friends was vital. Along with Carter, James was particularly close with fellow Akron natives Randy Mims and Richard Paul. They called themselves "The Four Horsemen," and even had jackets and jewelry made to reflect that moniker. Gilbert realized it was important to sell his vision of the franchise not just to the public . . . not just to James . . . but also The Horsemen.

There was another player, William "Wes" Wesley. He is a bit of a legend in NBA inner circles for being a major influence on some of the game's biggest name players. Wesley is affable and has an engaging personality. He has a confident air about him, yet is not cocky. He not only talks a good game, but he also can listen. Gilbert probably thought, "This guy would make a great broker for me at Quicken

Loans," when he met Wesley. The man had a way of becoming friends with high profile professional athletes, NBA executives, coaches, corporate sponsors and entertainers. His specialty is connecting and advising people. He operates like the investment giant Goldman Sachs; he introduces parties for new businesses. And yes, he has his favorites, people whom he knows and trusts—and he tells players about them. Because he has no official title, works for no company or team, Wesley is a mysterious figure. One thing is clear: he is paid very well by different clients for different services. He's known James since the St. Vincent-St. Mary days, making frequent trips to Akron. Wesley had ties with Cavs guard Dajuan Wagner, and that led to James. Wagner and James knew each other from the summer basketball circuit. During James' senior year, he attended some Cavs games with Wesley—who owned courtside season tickets. After James came to the Cavs, he moved into an apartment across the hall from Wesley in downtown Cleveland.

Wesley is close with two of James biggest heroes, Michael Jordan and hip-hop artist Shawn "Jay-Z" Carter. Wesley endeared himself to James in many ways, especially when he arranged for James to meet Jay-Z and his actress/singer girlfriend, Beyonce Knowles. Jay-Z and James later became friends. On the basketball court, with his Nikes and his No. 23, James very much wants to be like Jordan. Off the court, in his personal and business dealings, he very much wants to be like Jay-Z, who developed a business empire away from his music business. Wesley also owned a home in Detroit, where he was a regular in courtside seats at Pistons games and had become close with Pistons General Manager Joe Dumars and star guard Richard Hamilton. Both Hamilton and Wagner used agent Leon Rose, Wesley's longtime friend and attorney. In recent years, the media has picked up on Wesley's role in the game, especially following the infamous brawl at the Palace of Auburn Hills during a game between the Pistons and Indiana Pacers in 2005. He left his courtside seat and helped lead Pacers forward Ron Artest out of a fight in the stands and off the floor. In video footage seen over and over, Wesley held his hand over Artest's head while being pelted with beer and debris from the stands.

It was also in Detroit where Wesley met another soon-to-be NBA power, Gilbert, who was a major Pistons corporate sponsor before buying the Cavaliers. Not long after becoming the Cavs owner, Gilbert was reaching out to James' friends. They were guests in his courtside box during games, and they met and dined away from the court. Carter was even a guest on Gilbert's private jet. It was unorthodox, as owners usually do not hang out with star players so-called posses, even if Carter was technically an employee with Nike. But this was not some group of guys off the street sucking blood and dollars out of a player. The Horsemen are friends, advisors and in some areas, partners with James. Gilbert wisely recognized this, and treated these young men with respect as he developed a relationship.

Shortly after Gilbert took over the team, James fired Goodwin. Despite the more than $125 million in endorsements Goodwin had negotiated for him, James wanted Carter to run his marketing. Goodwin had been at odds with James' friends for at least a year, differing on some off-court decisions being made. Over the next few months, Carter became head of a marketing company created to handle James' endorsements. It was called LRMR, the first initials of each of The Four Horsemen. James hired Wesley's business partner Rose as his new basketball agent. Gilbert hired Mims, who had always traveled with James to road games, as a full-time employee. Later, Jay-Z even hired Paul to be a model for his clothing line. It was not uncommon at home games to see Rose, Wesley, Paul and Carter in courtside seats at the end of the Cavs bench, and sitting nearby was Mims. James' closest friends and advisors were often around him in a comfortable cocoon.

The 2005–06 season was the first full year under Gilbert, and it became the best of James' career. Playing with upgraded talent and under new coach Mike Brown, James flourished. With more shooters to help spread out defenses, James thrived on attacking the basket. Stronger and more seasoned and getting more respect from referees, he put up career highs, averaging 31.4 points a game and breaking every single-season scoring mark in team history. He won the All-Star Game Most Valuable Player Award when he scored 29 points in Houston. Down the stretch of the regular season, he thrived in close games by making a series of last-second shots and last-second decisions that helped the Cavs win 18 of their last 22 games. It earned them 50 wins, the most in 12 seasons, and a No. 4 overall seed in the Eastern Conference playoffs. He averaged 36 points per game and hit two last-second shots to win games in a first round playoff series win over the Washington Wizards, the Cavs first playoff series victory in 13 years. Led by a strong James performance in the second round, the Cavs pushed the top-seeded Detroit Pistons to seven games before losing out.

James was unanimously named First Team All-NBA and was second to Steve Nash in the season Most Valuable Player of the Year voting. New coach Mike Brown got votes for Coach of the Year and the Cavs rewarded him by extending his contract for a season. General Manager Danny Ferry said that after all the upheaval the year before, the team would not make many moves because it wanted some stability in the organization. It was then, at this happy and contented time, that Ferry, Gilbert and other Cavs officials visited James and offered him the contract extension in a meeting in the basement of Ken Stewart's restaurant in Akron.

Gilbert had been telling James and his friends, "We want to make the Cleveland Cavaliers the very best franchise in basketball—in all of sports. We want to be the place where everyone in the NBA wants to play."

Sound outrageous? So did making a little mortgage company in Livonia, Michigan, into a business on-line powerhouse. Yet another of Gilbert's rules in his company's handbook reads: "Think big, huge, large, enormous, gigantic, immense, jumbo king-sized, mammoth, massive, thundering."

He also says, "You'll see it when you believe it."

When Gilbert told James about his vision for the Cavaliers, the owner already saw it all in his head. James could actually see it in the arena and dressing room upgrades, along with the rest of the perks for players. He could feel it on the court, where Brown's defensive philosophy began to pay off in victories. He sensed it everywhere from fans and friends, who were excited about the Cavaliers and begging him to sign an extension as soon as possible.

"I felt comfortable that LeBron would sign," said Ferry. "We had won a round of the playoffs. We were starting to put our philosophy and culture in place. LeBron likes it here, this is where he wanted to stay."

The Cavs just had to give him reasons to stick around for more.

After taking a week to think about it and then having lunch to talk things over with Jay-Z in New York, James called the Cavs and told them he'd sign. Instead of signing the full five-year extension offer, he would sign for three years with his option for a fourth. By taking a shorter deal, James left about $20 million in guaranteed money on the table. The move, which was copied by James contemporaries Dwyane Wade and Chris Bosh when they signed their extensions days afterward, sent two messages. James was happy with things in Cleveland and the changes in the organization, and wanted to be there for the future. He also wanted the Cavs to know they could not become complacent. He is committed until the summer of 2010, but he wanted the team to keep moving in the right direction.

"I signed a deal that would make me the most comfortable," James said. "I'm happy to be a Cavalier and happy to be staying at home. I thought a lot about it and I did what was best for me."

"To his credit, we never heard from LeBron or anyone in his camp that he was interested in leaving," said Gilbert. "It's not like they were pounding the table and saying, 'We're staying for sure.' But they made it clear they wanted to be here. I'm always nervous until a deal like that is done, but I felt confident he'd stay."

It was a major victory for the Cavs organization, which had come so far in just a year. When he heard from Ferry that James had officially put his signature on the contract, Gilbert and his wife, Jennifer, had a celebratory bottle of wine. As it turned out, much bigger celebrations would follow.

CHAPTER 19

"THIS IS ALWAYS EVOLVING"

Plowing through the playoffs

As the Cavaliers gathered for their first practice of the 2006–07 season, there was a sense of comfort. Most of the faces were familiar and so was the system. Larry Hughes was pronounced healthy, the finger that needed two surgeries was working again. The coaching staff was intact from the year before, the starting lineup and top nine players in the rotation were virtually the same, and nearly everyone on the team was in a long-term contract.

It was something the Cavaliers had not experienced in years, something so basic, yet so shocking to this franchise. That something was stability, a key to victory, according to General Manager Danny Ferry.

Coach Mike Brown and his assistants spent the off season designing some new offensive sets and plays aimed at getting more players than James involved. There was confidence it would work along with a sense of excitement and optimism around the team. When the first practice broke, however, something happened that took just about everyone by surprise. In leading the huddle, LeBron James ended the workout by asking his teammates to chant championship in unison.

As is 1-2-3 . . . CHAMPIONSHIP!

It used to be 1-2-3 . . . DEFENSE!

That was Mike Brown's motto. But James wanted more, and the players were stunned by it. James seriously believed the Cavs could compete for an NBA title, and he wanted his teammates to be serious as well. After enjoying a cushy summer following the franchise's best season in more than a decade, James' actions were a reminder of the expectations.

"This isn't about pacing ourselves or just trying to make the playoffs anymore," James told reporters, who were equally taken back by the bold nature of his early-season chant. "At some point we've got to start putting up some banners in this building. I have signed to be here long term and this is my team. I am trying to win a championship here."

The previous summer, James was named one of the co-captains of the 2006 Team USA. The Americans and James played well at the World Championships outside Tokyo, but a bad 10-minute stretch against the Greeks cost them a game and they had to settle for the bronze medal. After the sixth place finish at the 2002 Worlds and a bronze at the 2004 Olympics, it was more shame for the once mighty Americans. But James took a lot from the experience as a leader and was showing it early in the season. And he was right, his Cavaliers were going to be very high, at least Eastern Conference Finals high. The Cavs were a preseason pick to challenge the defending champion Miami Heat and the Detroit Pistons for the East title. James was a hot prediction for Most Valuable Player.

Much of this was validated in the first game of the season at San Antonio. On national television, the Cavs and James came out and took down the three-time champions. It was the first time they'd won in San Antonio since 1988. James was masterful, scoring 35 points with 10 rebounds. He made a series of athletic moves to the basket including a dunk over the top of Spurs two-time MVP Tim Duncan, which proved to be one of the highlights of the year in the NBA. After getting home from the road trip, Mark Cashman, the Cavs equipment manager, took a still image of the dunk and put it above James locker. It stayed there, its edges fraying and turning up, until the end of the season. This was the Spurs home opener, and *San Antonio Express-News* writer Buck Harvey's column the next day opened with: "LeBron James showed up for the Spurs first home game. But what happens if he's here for the last one?" Harvey knew the Spurs were title contenders and after seeing James and the Cavs, he boldly suggested the two teams could be meeting again some seven months later.

Who knew Harvey would be right?

Not many around the Cavaliers, especially in the eighth game of the season as they were on a five-game winning streak, blowing out the hapless Portland Trail Blazers in Cleveland. Midway through the second quarter as Larry Hughes fought for a rebound, Portland forward Martell Webster fell on Hughes from behind. Hughes crashed to the floor and immediately reached for his lower right leg. The crowd was silent. It was a freak occurrence, but a year before, when Hughes got his hand caught in someone's jersey in a preseason game in Milwaukee, it cost him 45 games. Freak injury, fractured finger. Things like that seem to keep happening to Hughes during his career, and that finger required two surgeries and had a major impact on the season. So did this twist of fate. Hughes hobbled off to get x-rays. By the second half he was back on the bench and the scoreboard announced to the fans his leg injury was not believed to be serious. He told reporters after the game that he hoped to play in the next game. The Cavs listed him as day-to-day on their injury report.

The truth, though, was much more grim. An MRI revealed that Hughes had a high ankle sprain, the sort that takes months to heal. He sat out 10 games and the Cavs went 5-5 after previously having the best record in the Eastern Conference. He rushed back not having anywhere near full strength in the ankle. Hughes often landed only on his left foot after jumping, which affected his shot and ultimately caused him to develop tendinitis in his left leg. His whole game suffered as his scoring, shooting and rebounding all dropped. For several months, he couldn't even dunk the ball.

It wasn't just Hughes. James also was dealing with some issues. He fervently denied he felt any fatigue from the six weeks he spent in the Far East playing exhibitions and in the World Championships over the summer, but his performance showed otherwise. He had several big games, like the night in San Antonio, but overall his performance was not on the same level as the previous season. His shooting and scoring were down. Brown was working on getting him more rest during and between games, even letting him sit out some practices. But some nights he just seemed to have low energy; in several Cavs losses he didn't even score a point in the fourth quarter. The season before, he'd led the Eastern Conference in fourth-quarter scoring. On December

30, the Cavs blew a fourth-quarter lead in Chicago and lost as their record slid to 17-12. The first two months of the season were the two easiest for the Cavs in terms of schedule. They hadn't taken advantage, partly due to Hughes' injury, partly due to James not carrying them to more victories as he'd done regularly the year before. The Cavs were still competing for first place in the Central Division, but from the front office to the coaching staff to the players to the media and fans, all were asking the same question: "Why aren't they better?"

The team started January with a five-game win streak, which looked like it might turn things around. But they finished the month losing seven of 11 games, staggering through a rough seven-game West Coast trip. That made them 9-7 for the first month of 2007, hardly the sign of a strong playoff run. More likely, it seemed storm clouds were forming.

In early February, the Cavs blew a huge lead in Miami to lose to the Heat. Then they were humbled by 12 points on their home floor by the Detroit Pistons on national television on Super Bowl Sunday. The Cavs had lost eight of 12 games and sank to fifth place in the Eastern Conference. After starting the season, the team was just 20-19, nearly a half season of being just average. They were playing great defense, ranking in the top 10 in the league in most categories. But the offense that looked good on paper with all the Xs and Os—it broke down under the pressure of the regular season. James was left dribbling and shooting bad jumpers when plays stopped, which seemed to happen often against good teams like the Pistons and in so many key situations. After scoring just 78 points against the Pistons, the frustration poured out. Brown, who had worked hard to develop a no excuses rule within the team, blasted the officials for calling too few fouls on the Pistons. It was his way of lashing out. The players aimed at a different target. A day after the loss to Detroit, James and Hughes told reporters they were tired of the Cavs' slow-down style of offense and wanted to run more. They wanted to quicken the pace of the game in an attempt to put up more points. They hinted the current style wouldn't let them.

"We can be a good defensive team and play in the half-court," James said. "But at the end of the day, if you don't put points on the board, you're not going to win basketball games. At times it is fun to get up and down and throw lobs. I've probably caught two lobs this year and that's a career low."

It was a direct challenge to Brown, who had spent the last season and a half trying to get his team to commit to defense first. Now, his team leaders were talking about playing a more fun offense. It was a crisis for the young head coach, who was facing his first giant crossroads. When pressed by the media for a response, he said "I don't believe in making changes, but I do believe in making tweaks. This is always evolving."

That statement swung both ways. After the comments hit the press, Brown held a team meeting. He told them they could do whatever they wanted on offense, break plays, run, dunk, whatever, just as long as they continued playing good defense. This was Brown's style. He's not a commanding, disciplinarian coach. He tried to form partnerships with his players. By putting the responsibility of the offense in their hands, he was demanding they take some ownership for what was happening on the court. If it worked, they would appreciate him giving them freedom. If it didn't, he felt like the players would take the responsibility themselves.

But he did indeed make some adjustments. In a move that he'd been thinking about for weeks, he replaced captain Eric Snow with rookie Daniel Gibson in the starting lineup at point guard. Snow was a better defender, but Gibson had proven to be one of the teams best shooters. Because of his practice performance, Gibson had won the faith and approval of James, who'd been pushing for the guard to get more playing time. Brown also decreased the minutes of veteran guard Damon Jones in favor of Sasha Pavlovic, a taller and more athletic swingman. Brown had finally convinced Pavlovic to play some defense after a year and a half of benchings.

Whether it was a change in the lineup or the change in the tactics, the Cavs began to regroup and move in a positive direction. With Gibson in the starting lineup the Cavs broke out of the slump and went 8-5 before a toe injury sidelined the rookie. Gibson was injured in a narrow loss in Dallas to the NBA-best Mavericks at the start of March. The Cavs played one of their best games of the season against the Mavericks and still lost. James put up 39 points but missed a 3-pointer at the buzzer that could've tied the game. The difference in this loss was that the Cavs left feeling good about themselves and their future. It had taken Dallas' best game to beat them at home without Gibson and without Hughes, who missed the game with a stomach flu. To replace Gibson, instead of going back to Snow, Brown decided to make Hughes the starting point guard and Pavlovic the starter at shooting guard. This turned out to complete the turnaround. With his ankle finally starting to heal, Hughes had direct control of the offense with James, which is what they both wanted. It carried over on defense as the Cavs found a stride. They won the first eight games Hughes started at point guard, and increased their scoring average nearly four points a game. James began playing like an MVP again, averaging 30 points over a 20-game stretch to earn NBA Player of the Month honors in March. Still, the push nearly came too late.

Despite finishing the season by winning 17-of-24 games, the Cavs' long stretch of subpar play had taken a toll in the standings. They missed out on a chance to catch Detroit for the Central Division title. They also were dueling the Bulls for second place. They didn't own the tiebreakers because of their poor play against conference opponents earlier in the season. On the last night of the season, the Cavs beat the Milwaukee Bucks to post their second straight 50-32 season. Despite having the second-best record in the conference, they were staring at getting the No. 5 playoff seed due to tiebreakers. That would've put them in a first-round match-up with the defending champion Heat— and then a potential date with the Pistons in the second round. After the game ended, the Cavs players hurried into the locker room to watch the Bulls play the New Jersey Nets. The Cavs needed the Nets to beat Chicago in order for Cleveland to secure the coveted second playoff seed. The players celebrated as the Nets won the game, leaving the Bulls at 49-33 and the Cavs as the No. 2 seed for the playoffs. With all the injuries, lineup switches and internal turmoil, the Cavs ended up with their highest seed ever in the 16-team playoff format.

Now, the real season was about to begin—and the pressure the most James and this group of Cavaliers had ever felt.

CHAPTER 20

GETTING THERE

The first trip to the finals

From behind the bench and without saying a word, Cavs assistant trainer Mike Mancias placed a towel soaked in ice water on the back of LeBron James' wide neck. Another towel was draped over his sweat-soaked shoulders as he hung his head, staring at the floor. Teammates inched over or stood up, allowing him to sprawl across three folding chairs next to the floor at the Palace of Auburn Hills. The horn sounded inside the muggy arena, which was filled with tension after the Pistons and Cavs had played to a draw over more than 57 intense minutes. James' head rose and he grimaced, shedding his layers of towels and emerging from the huddle around the bench area. He fixed his eyes on the court and in one motion flung his shoulders back, straightening his uniform, and walked intently back onto the court. There were 20 seconds left in double overtime. Once again, the play was called for James. It had been like that for the last hour. Get the ball to LeBron and get out of the way. Never had he been so hot, and not just because of the sweat pouring off his body. He believed every time he shot the ball—from everywhere and anywhere—it was going through the hoop. He had scored 23 straight points for the Cavs, and 27 of the last 28. He had made driving dunks and twisting lay-ups, jumpers from the right side, left side and top of the key. He burned his man one-on-one, split double teams, and bulled through triple teams to do it.

James had already amassed a remarkable playoff record. In 2006, he carried the Cavs past the Washington Wizards in the first round—and nearly upset these same top-ranked Pistons in the second round.

But this postseason trip was even better. He averaged 28 points a game in the first round, wiping out the Wizards in a four-game sweep. In the second round, he'd led the Cavs to a 4-2 series win over the New Jersey Nets, his 30 points in Game 4 landing the Cavs a two-point victory. Then in the clincher, Game 6 at the Meadowlands in New Jersey, James scored 14 points in the first quarter to jump out to a massive lead they never let go.

On to the Eastern Conference Finals against Detroit.

James was involved in last-second plays that decided the first two games. In Game 1, with the Cavs down by two points with the ball in the final seconds, he chose to pass to teammate Donyell Marshall for what would've been a game-winning 3-pointer. Marshall had been a hero in the series against the Nets with his 3-point makes—only in Detroit, he missed a wide-open 20-footer from the corner. That's Marshall's favorite shooting spot, and James knew it. James took heat from fans and media who thought he should not have passed, a recurring issue with him over the years. On one hand, James was known as the Cavs' best player and praised for leading the team in assists in each of his first four years. On the other, some felt he needed to be the one to decide close games, not his lesser teammates. Force up some big shots rather than rely on teammates who were open. Supposedly, that's what great players do, at least according to the critics of James.

In Game 2, it was the same situation. The Cavs were behind by two points in the closing seconds, and James decided to keep the ball. He forced a shot against a double team and missed, even as replays showed he was fouled on the play. James was feeling the pressure to deliver, and had to cope with the media attacks that he had failed once again in the clutch as the Cavs were behind 0-2 in this best-of-7 series.

Back at Quicken Loans Arena for Game 3, James arrived three hours early to practice by himself before more than 20,000 empty seats. He wanted to be on the floor before fans were admitted so he could work on his shooting and work out some nervous energy. An hour before the tip, he held his customary meeting with the media and declared it was the "most important game of my life." He played with that intensity, scoring 32 points with nine rebounds and nine assists to carry the Cavs to victory and back into the series. Two days later, he had 25 points and 11 assists, trusting his teammates to take down the Pistons' defensive coverages as the Cavs won to tie the series at 2-2.

That led to the sweltering May night at the Palace of Auburn Hills, outside Detroit. While it was the Cavs vs. Pistons, this was seen as the 22-year-old's chance to make his first major statement to the league. Could James carry his team past a better, more experienced opponent? The NBA is a league based on stars, which was why there was so much excitement over the Akron native since he was a young teenager. But games such as this one were why scouts raved about James, why the shoe companies bid for him and why teams brought lucky charms to the LeBron Lottery. This was to be his moment, his night, his true coming out party as a legitimate, prime time playoff NBA superstar.

James took the inbounds pass and started dribbling at the top of the key as the crowd tensed, coming to the edge of their seats, hearts pounding, voices raw and screeching. James drove left past Pistons' star Chauncey Billups, one of the four men the Pistons tried to use as defenders on James over the long, intense Game 5. James jumped in the air, slipping in between defenders Jason Maxiell and Tayshuan Prince. He needed every ounce of his enormous strength, speed and athleticism. Creating space, he flipped the ball underhanded off the glass and through the rim for the winning basket. James had scored 48 points, notching every point the Cavs scored in the last 18 minutes of the game. He scored every point in both overtimes, leaving even his teammates and his opponents looking at each other in disbelief. The entire arena knew he was going to shoot and it seemed the Pistons ran all five defenders at him on some plays—but it didn't matter. He knew he'd score, and he knew no one would stop him. The Pistons and their fans knew it, too.

Right after the game, the arena was nearly silent but the raves for James were just beginning. Cavs and basketball fans in general were emotional about the game's events. Within minutes, TNT commentators Charles Barkley and Kenny Smith debated where the performance ranked all-time, a conversation that lasted for days. Was it the best ever, or just one of the best ever? Either way, greatness had appeared in the person of James in his No. 23 Cavaliers jersey. And there was no doubt about this: While the Cavs were once down 0-2 in this series as their star was unable to come through in the clutch—now they had charged to a 3-2 series lead. They were one win away from their first Eastern Conference championship in franchise history.

"I'm tired, I'm sore, I'm banged up, I'm winded, I feel terrible," James said after the game, needing intravenous fluids before he boarded the team flight home.

Was he surprised by how the Cavs had come back, and how he performed under pressure?

"But I'm not surprised," he said. "Why should I be surprised?"

From the first day of practice nearly eight months before. James was talking about a championship. He thought it was possible. With his weeks of tremendous playoff performances, he'd made it a possibility. Then, he made it a reality.

Two nights later, the Cavs earned themselves a banner. On the night the Cavs drafted James in June of 2003, he said he planned to "light up Cleveland like Las Vegas." Four years later, he came pretty close. Facing a streaking James and the confident Cavs, the Pistons were unable to change the momentum in Game 6. The night of June 2, 2007, was the first game ever played in the month of June in Cavs history. It became perhaps the most memorable moment in the 37-year history of the franchise. The somewhat embarrassed Pistons decided they were not going to let James beat them. They sent double-teams his way, two men rushing to defend James even when he was 25 feet from the basket. It creates chances for others to star, and they did. Rookie Daniel Gibson had won over the Cavs in private workouts the previous summer. Then he impressed James in early season workouts. In this Game 6, he swished five 3-pointers and scored a career-high 31 points. Gibson scored 19 in the fourth quarter as the Cavs turned a close game into a blowout and a spot in their first-ever NBA Finals.

The last time a major professional team from Cleveland had won a league title was in 1964 when the Cleveland Browns beat the Baltimore Colts in the NFL Championship. Twice since, in 1995 and 1997, the Cleveland Indians reached the World Series. Both times the Indians won the pennant it happened out of town. This moment happened in Cleveland, and was magnified by tens of thousands of fans who were in the streets around the arena, most staying around after a sold out Indians game the same night at nearby Jacobs Field. The streets around the arena were shut down as fans celebrated in them, horns blared and cameras flashed. It wasn't a title, but it was the closest thing to celebrate for the Cavs since the franchise began in 1970. In the arena, James flung the game ball into the air as the game ended. First into his arms was Zydrunas Ilgauskas, the veteran center who James campaigned to re-sign two years before. Ilgauskas had endured a difficult season personally. His wife Jennifer had miscarried twins at midseason and both were still very much in mourning. Ilgauskas said the celebrations from the Cavs postseason run helped in the couple's healing process.

The next man to reach James was even an older friend, Eddie Jackson. The father figure who helped advise him and support him in high school, Jackson rushed from his courtside seat and embraced James at center court. Within seconds, James was swallowed by teammates as he pulled on a T-shirt and hat announcing the Cavs as Eastern Conference champions. A few moments later, NBA Hall of Famer Bill Russell handed Cavs owner Dan Gilbert the Eastern Conference championship trophy. It had been two years and two months since he'd taken control of the team. Then Russell, the winner of 11 NBA championships with the Boston Celtics, turned to James and said, "You are a year younger than me when we won our first Eastern Conference championship."

James shyly smiled and nodded, a rare moment of being humbled. The Cavs were only the third team in NBA history to win a conference finals series after falling down 0-2. That night turned out to be the peak of the Cavs' season, the greatest season in team history. Next up were the San Antonio Spurs, who had the home-court advantage and the experience advantage. Their core had won two NBA titles already. Their star, Tim Duncan, had won three. Cavs General Manager Danny Ferry had shared in two of the titles, head coach Mike Brown had shared in one. It was the students meeting the teachers.

The Cavs were wounded. Larry Hughes had torn tissue in his foot in Game 4 against the Pistons. He took painkilling injections to get through games, but he couldn't keep up with Spurs super-quick point guard Tony Parker. After two NBA Finals games, Hughes could no longer stand the pain and moved to the bench.

The Spurs' defensive tactics were superior to those of the Pistons and the Nets before them. They allowed James to have space to move—but only for jump shots. Suddenly, James' jumpers were unreliable. He had trouble finding a clear path to drive to the basket. He shot just 36 percent in the series, and the Cavs offense couldn't recover. Parker played at his highest level, averaged nearly 25 points in the series while shooting 57 percent from the floor and 58 percent on 3-pointers. Duncan averaged 18 points and 12 rebounds. Manu Ginobili, the Spurs' third star, averaged 18 points. Games 1 and 2 went easily to the Spurs in San Antonio. At Quicken Loans Arena, Game 3 was decided by three points and Game 4 was decided by one point. But it was still a San Antonio sweep, the Spurs claiming their fourth championship in nine years. For the Cavs and James, the ultimate prize would have to wait.

A few moments after the game, as the Spurs were celebrating in the visitor's locker room, James entered the interview room to speak to the media.

"We did what we said we could do, make it to the championship and tried to win the championship," he said. "We wanted to win the big thing and we're going to keep trying. We have to get better. I have to get better."

In the hallway, James ran into Duncan, who was holding the championship trophy. The Spurs star pulled James close and whispered into his ear.

"Someday this league is going to belong to you," Duncan said.

As James left the building that night, beaten but determined, it was not hard to share Duncan's vision.

ACKNOWLEDGMENTS

BRIAN WINDHORST:

Thanks to Aaron Goodwin, Sonny Vaccaro, Fred Schreyer, Chris Rivers, Chris Dennis, Calvin Andrews, Gordon Gund, Jim Paxson and Paul Silas. And special thanks to Terry Pluto, Tom Reed and Royce Webb for their long-term help in making me a better writer.

TERRY PLUTO:

This was not a quick book written just because the Cavs made the NBA finals. It was a two-year project. In addition to the people Brian mentions above, I'd like to thank Danny Ferry, Mike Brown, Dan Gilbert, Mark Warkentein, Tad Carper, researches Geoff Beckman and Wally Mieskoski, and copyeditor Eric Broder. Also, thanks to David Gray for his confidence in this project and to Chris Andrikanich and Jane Lassar, who are a great support to me.

OTHER BOOKS OF INTEREST . . .

LeBron James: The Rise of a Star
David Lee Morgan Jr.

From high school hoops to #1 NBA draft pick. An inside look at LeBron James's youth and high school years, when he was basketball's hottest young prospect, poised at the brink of superstardom. Sportswriter David Lee Morgan covered the LeBron phenomenon from the begining and had unequaled access to LeBron, his family, and his close friends.

"A well-rounded, personal portrait of the young superstar"
– Booklist

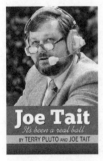

Joe Tait: It's Been a Real Ball
Stories from a Hall-of-Fame Sports Broadcasting Career

Terry Pluto, Joe Tait

Legendary broadcaster Joe Tait is like an old family friend to three generations of Cleveland sports fans. This book celebrates the inspiring career of "the Voice of the Cleveland Cavaliers" with stories from Joe and dozens of fans, colleagues, and players. Hits the highlights of a long career and also uncovers some touching personal details.

"An easy, fun book to read and will surely bring back good memories for Cleveland sports fans who listened to Tait's trademark calls since 1970."
– 20SecondTimeout.com

Dealing
The Cleveland Indians' New Ballgame: How a Small-Market Team Reinvented Itself as a Major League Contender

Terry Pluto

An in-depth, inside look at how the Cleveland Indians' front office took their team apart and rebuilt to become contenders again in spite of modern baseball's competitive imbalance. Veteran sportswriter Terry Pluto had unprecedented access. He delivers a wealth of detail that will intrigue serious fans and fantasy leaguers.

Read samples at **www.grayco.com**

OTHER BOOKS OF INTEREST . . .

Things I've Learned from Watching the Browns
Terry Pluto

Veteran sports writer Terry Pluto asks Cleveland Browns fans: Why, after four decades of heartbreak, teasing, and futility, do you still stick with this team? Their stories, coupled with Pluto's own insight and analysis, deliver the answers. Like any intense relationship, it's complicated. But these fans just won't give up.

"For dedicated Browns fans [the book is] like leafing through an old family photo album." – BlogCritics.com

Glory Days in Tribe Town
The Cleveland Indians and Jacobs Field 1994–1997
Terry Pluto, Tom Hamilton

Relive the most thrilling seasons of Indians baseball in recent memory! Cleveland's top sportswriter teams up with the Tribe's veteran radio announcer and fans to share favorite stories from the first years of Jacobs Field, when a star-studded roster (Belle, Thome, Vizquel, Ramirez, Alomar, Nagy) and a sparkling ballpark captivated an entire city.

The Top 20 Moments in Cleveland Sports
Tremendous Tales of Heroes and Heartbreaks
Bob Dyer

Relive the most memorable and sensational events in Cleveland sports history. Many of them are known by shorthand: Red Right 88. The Drive. The Fumble. The Shot. Beer Night. Some were gut-wrenching. Some, like the 1964 NFL championship game, were glorious. All are highlight of the shared experience of all Cleveland sports fans.

Read samples at **www.grayco.com**